Collection « Socio-anthropologie des mondes méditerranéens et africains »

Cette collection, fondée et dirigée par Pierre-Noël Denieuil, s'attache à valoriser et à diffuser les travaux de chercheurs en sciences humaines et sociales, portant sur les territoires méditerranéens : Maghreb, Proche-Orient, rives nord et sud-est de la Méditerranée.

La dimension socio-anthropologique est le garant d'une attention portée aux populations, à leurs usages, à leurs systèmes de valeurs et au lien social qui structurent un projet de société. Cette perspective peut judicieusement se superposer avec des approches historique, juridique, politologique et économique des mondes concernés.

Sur les bases géographiques et disciplinaires ci-dessus décrites, la collection abrite des thématiques aussi variées et complémentaires que : monde rural et agricole ; dynamiques urbaines ; entrepreneuriat et accès à l'emploi ; développement social, sociabilités et solidarités ; politiques publiques et espaces privés ; réformes et réformisme ; socio-anthropologie du droit ; sociologies de la santé ; recompositions de la famille.

Ces travaux peuvent être monographiques (axés sur un pays en particulier) ou plus précisément comparatifs (approches croisées sur les sociétés, analyse des interdépendances entre les deux rives).

5-7, rue de l'École polytechnique, 75005 Paris

www.harmattan.fr

ISBN : 978-2-343-23175-4
EAN : 9782343231754

Fall to the abyss

Tunisia from revolution to pandemic

Houda Laroussi

Fall to the abyss

Tunisia from revolution to pandemic

L'Harmattan

BY THE SAME AUTHOR

La Tunisie en pandémie. De la corruption à la solidarité, 120 pages, L'Harmattan, Paris, 2021.

Les descendants d'immigrés tunisiens en France et en Tunisie. La relation des deux rives, (en collaboration avec Pierre-Noel Denieuil, Sonia El Amdouni, Radhia Mechken, Makrem Mandhouj et Nouha Doudech), 455 pages, Nirvana, Tunis, 2019.

Femmes et développement local en Tunisie, 180 pages, L'Harmattan, Paris, 2018.

Pratiques du travail social en France et au Maghreb (direction d'ouvrage), 339 pages, L'Harmattan, Paris, 2017.

Tunisie 2011-2014. Radioscopie d'une entrée en révolution (en collaboration avec Pierre-Noël Denieuil), 181 pages, L'Harmattan-CRDI-OJT, Paris-Tunis, 2017.

Le prêt sur gage au Crédit municipal de Paris. Clientèle et mondes sociaux, 302 pages, Karthala, Paris, 2012.

Micro-crédit et lien social en Tunisie. La solidarité instituée, 352 pages, Karthala, Paris, 2009.

Le développement social local et la question des territoires (en collaboration avec Pierre-Noël Denieuil), 271 pages, L'Harmattan, Paris, 2005.

INTRODUCTION

The 2020 epidemic crisis

This book was written during the first period of confinement in Tunisia, from March to June 2020[1]. Its materials were mainly our paper readings, our browsing on the net, some exchanges with our relatives, as well as the memory and knowledge of our own research work. The text that follows is voluntarily dated over a period which was subsequently extended, which experienced the twists and turns we know (multiplicity of waves of Covid 19), which remains today in progress, and which marked the beginning of a new world. This text is characterized by its appearance as a response to a state of confinement and immobilization, an exploratory personal essay on a subject that concerns us all. It is an attempt to understand and put it into a global perspective in an international context, and with Tunisia as a focal point. It takes into account, however, with caution and the necessary conditionalities with regard to the data collected, particularly geopolitical information, widely relayed on digital networks and often not readily available in the official press and in studies commissioned by institutions.

[1] I would like to thank Mr. Mohamed S. F. to translate this book, originally written in French. The quotes given throughout the text when they came from documents consulted in French and cited in a note in their French edition, have been translated.

The virus that concerns us is not specific to a country, it is precisely one of the manifestations of globalization, deliberately cross-border. It did not fall from the sky, it was built and passed on internaltional. The governments and decision-makers who are confronted with it oppose rules, reforms, policies. But its current geographic influence all over the world is part of a historical dimension. Indeed, since the beginnings of humanity, viruses and pandemics have raged, have decimated populations, have undergone economic changes and social upheavals, have often been instrumentalized by the institutions and policies of the countries concerned, bordering or colonizing, or even served as the fall of empires or the decline of societies.

The Coronavirus, an unsolved enigma

The Corona virus spread in December 2019 to form part of a global pandemic. The majority of affected countries did not estimate its extent and speed of spread. As soon as it first appeared, the virus was underestimated because of its asymptomatic or benign nature in the majority of people affected. During this first wave, we asked ourselves several questions dealing with the spread of the virus and the modalities of its treatment.

The coronavirus family includes 6 viruses that infect humans. Four of them (OC43, HKU1, NL63 and 229E) bother the individual, causing a third of the common cold. The other two viruses are MERS (Middle East Respiratory Syndrome Coronavirus) and SARS (Severe Acute Respiratory Syndrome). Epidemiological researchers point out that the Corona virus, which has existed for centuries, is very abundant in animals[2]. Of many aspects of this

[2] Infection of a person through direct contact with infected animals or contaminated environments does not lead to efficient transmission of the virus to humans. There is no indication that a person can be infected with avian or

Corona 19 virus are still unknown because it causes a disease with symptoms different from the flu, it spreads easily and kills quickly. The shape of the virus is spherical, with spines or pods, containing the protein called ACE2. According to experts, the temperature would not affect it, and it could affect young people, however often asymptomatic but nonetheless carriers in people at risk or over 65 years. The affected person will not necessarily fall ill during the first few days of being infected, and some will not even experience any symptoms. The incubation period varies greatly from person to person, but is on average five days. The virus mainly needs living bodies, but can nevertheless survive for more than seven days on surfaces. There is, however, a chance that it could be wiped out by washing with soap.

It is characterized by disorders of the respiratory system, spreads rapidly through the air by small invisible bacteria, and its contamination occurs through proximity between people or through infected surfaces. It would first reach the cells of the throat, the windpipe and then the lungs. Upper respiratory tract infection can be transmitted easily, it is mild, while lower respiratory tract infection is more difficult to transmit, but it is more serious and causes difficulty in breathing. Chinese researchers at Sichuan University have reportedly shown that covid-19 does not attack the respiratory tract but rather the bloodstream. The lungs of patients with the virus are said to function normally and it is in fact the ability of red blood cells to carry oxygen that is affected by blocking the metabolism of the haem that takes in oxygen. Effects on the lungs that are identi-fied on scanners would be the result of an

---

animal influenza viruses through properly cooked food. However, the majority of human infections with the A H5N1 and A H7N9 viruses have been associated with direct or indirect contact with poultry infected alive or dead. Control of disease at the animal source level is essential to reduce human exposure to the risk of infection.

inflammatory reaction that would give these aspects on the images. If this study turns out to be true, the use of artificial respirators would be completely unnecessary. The challenge would then be to equip oneself with blood purification devices. Recent research shows that not all people with coronavirus have fully recovered from the disease, some have been exposed to the virus again and may even die. Contrary to what some researchers have mentioned in this area (it is said in the spring of 2020 that the vaccine will not appear in the short term), a vaccine has emerged and is now widely practiced around the world.

The virus's first repercussions on the global economy

The pandemic we are currently experiencing is nothing new, and is part of the course of the history of our humanity. Despite our scientific progress, we remain like previous societies, faced with a danger about which we do not know much, we are in ambiguity about its origins, its duration of action, and its forms of propagation.

In 6 months, the virus struck more than 208 countries around the world, infected more than three million people, caused the death of thousands of victims, and millions of students dropped out of schools around the world for fear of contamination. Likewise, hundreds of sporting and cultural events have been canceled, many places of worship have been closed to Muslims, Christians and Jews, as well as places of entertainment, theaters and cinema. Airlines anud trains have canceled flights for fear of the spread of the virus, layoffs of thousands of workers and losses of billions have been recorded, economic and productive sectors are contracted and billions of dollars have been lost in the financial markets have fallen.

The Coronavirus, after affecting thousands of people in China, has moved and radically changed the world economy and the order of international financial markets. All of this has translated into a deep economic recession and weak global trade. Even more severe effects are expected on the world economy for the coming decade. The recovery of an interconnected economy will not be immediate, it will need to be slowed down by governments, businesses and individuals, and will depend on the ability of the health sectors to bring the pandemic under control. In the European Union, the Paris and Frankfurt stock exchanges fell by more than 10% during the month of April after the European Central Bank unveiled a series of measures to support the economy of the euro zone, without, however, deliberately reducing interest rates. The CAC 40 index fell 10.2%, while the DAX 30 index in Frankfurt fell 10.3%. Also in April, European markets saw continued deterioration after Donald Trump announced the suspension of all flights between Europe and the United States for 30 days. Trading was halted on the New York Stock Exchange after it opened for 15 minutes for the second time during the week of April 13. The Dow Jones Index was down 7.20% and the Nasdaq Index, which was dominated by shares of technology companies, was down 7.03%. In Tokyo, the Nikkei is down 4.41%, losing more than 20% since the start of the year. The yen, a safe haven for investors, rose significantly against the dollar and the euro, a development very unfavorable for the Japanese export groups.

In the Arab world, Gulf stock exchanges recorded trading losses on Thursday, April 16 after two days of recovery, following an escalation in the oil which caused the drop in prices. For its part, the Saudi stock exchange, Tadawul, fell 3% in the last trading days before the weekend, while the shares of oil giant Aramco lost 2.4%

of their value four days before publishing the annual results. Significant losses were recorded in the United Arab Emirates, with the Dubai market index falling by 8% and Abu Dhabi by 7.4%. Likewise over the same period, the Qatar Stock Exchange fell 4.5%, the Oman market fell over 3% and the Bahrain market fell over 2%, while the Kuwait Stock Exchange remained closed.

A revealer of the crisis and of a new world order

The corona virus crisis reveals the emergence of another world order by questioning its social order (distancing, family withdrawal), health (health and safety in question), economic (shutdown of businesses, telework), financial (collapse of markets, fall of stock markets), and political (weakening of States, political indecision). It is at the origin of a new debate: the dilemma between preserving the economy or protecting health, developing goods opreserving people. There is a balance to be struck between the two options, human health or money. Some countries in the North have the means to circumvent the financial crisis, others in the South do not.

In this book, we wanted to shed light on the impact of the pandemic on our societies. We have equated the economic and social crisis that has plagued the world since the onset of the pandemic to a radical change, if not an unprecedented turn in the history of the economy. We have called it « Coronavirage », a concept proposed by the Tunisian sociallogue Abdelkhalek B'Chir. This Coronavirage is an opportunity for us to look into this new world order which is today becoming the frame of reference in which we operate, particularly in Tunisia. We have focused both on the health crisis and on the new experience that the majority of people are going through. The Coronavirus has been a good indicator of the crisis in certain Maghrebian societies, notably Algeria, Morocco and Tunisia. These three countries have experienced popular uprisings and social and political protest movements over the past ten years. The repercussions of the Covid on these companies converge to reinforce practices of speculation and trafficking, in particular of useful food products during periods of confinement. We thus find ourselves caught between this new international order and the need for radical change. The Tunisian economy, through the prism of this crisis, must seize the opportunity to change and move towards more harmonious social development, reconciling its antagonisms, poor and rich, young and senior, public, private and informal sector.

In the first part, The virus operator of change, we situate it in the context of all global pandemics and beyond borders. These pandemics, however less and less deadly, have introduced many changes in societies and created multiple interdependencies between them, sometimes benefiting the colonizer. The corona virus has become a social phenomenon that deeply imprints individual and collective behavior. While it generates social distancing, it can also be a producer of solidarity and human bond, as well as innovation with distance education and teleworking. It is also an opportunity for governments to enact new rules and must arouse the vigilance of citizens. Finally, we will see that the economic crisis which affects Algeria, Morocco and Tunisia, has induced new practices of small corruption and speculation in contexts of financial and banking fragility.

In a second part, Geopolitics of the New International Order, we address the new context of Arab and Maghreb countries until 2020. We situate the coronavirus crisis in the context of the collapse of world trade, and the financial crisis and stock market rife there. We consider first of all the United States as regulators of the world order on the one hand through their interference in world affairs, from South America to Asia, and on the other hand within the framework of 'a project for an « American military base » in southern Tunisia. Then we continue our survey of the weakening of Europe by the pandemic, to the supremacy now taken by China. Finally, this part ends with a brief review of the main networks of international influences nowadays present in Tunisia.

In a third part, Corruption in all its dimensions, we describe some ideal types of corruption in Tunisia, from financial and family corruption at the top of the state, to commercial transactions of petty corruption on the black market and at the same time, monopolies and money laundering. Finally, we are laying the groundwork for the constitution in Tunisia of a university center for research on corruption. We offer in turn: a project to document and capitalize on what already exists, the approaches to be implemented to better "understand" and explain corruption, then some proposals for studies or research themes to be carried out.

In our last part, The Curriculum of Social and Solidarity Economy CUR'ESS, in a Tunisia dominated by unemployment and informal practices, we would like to advocate a new model, that of the social and solidarity economy. In this perspective, we will return to the experience of cooperation or "reciprocity" to use Ahmed Ben Salah's term, in order to understand the modalities and development of this experience in the history of Tunisia. We will discuss the roots of the social economy and solidarity through Algerian and Tunisian experiences. Then we will present the main thrusts of a new project for Tunisia, both in the concrete objectives that should govern its establishment, and around the suggestion of strategic proposals for the revival of the economy within the framework of of CUR'ESS. This new project would take place in Tunisia in the construction of a third sector, capable of absorbing the so-called informal economy, and would complement the public and private sectors.

FIRST PART

The virus operator of changes

We will see below on the one hand that epidemics have no borders, on the other hand that we must consider the corona virus in its scale as a social phenomenon. Finally, we will discuss the development of the crisis and the rise in speculation in Algeria, Morocco and Tunisia.

1. EPIDEMICS BEYOND BORDERS

Throughout the history of mankind, epidemics - plague, cholera, influenza - have ravaged entire countries and caused enormous damage. These diseases, triggered by microscopic creatures unidentifiable by humans, have claimed more lives than any war. They killed millions of people. The Justinian Plague killed between 30 and 50 million people in the 6th century, equivalent to half of the world's population at the time. The virus struck the Byzantine Empire, in particular its capital, Constantinople, as well as the Sassanid Empire and coastal towns throughout the Mediterranean, where merchant ships harbored rats carrying plague-infected fleas.

Recall that the most important in history, « the black death or the black plague » reached three continents in 14th century between 1347 and 1351 and resulted in the death of nearly 200 million people in North Africa, Asia and Europe (or on this continent about a third of the total population).

In 1720, the great plague of Marseilles killed around 100,000 people, and a hundred years later, in 1820, Cholera killed more than 130,000 people in Indonesia, Thailand and the Philippines. In 1920 the Spanish flu killed nearly 50 million people, while around 500 million people around the world were infected. These epidemics have caused further damage as a large part of their populations has been confined to confined and contaminated places, such as schools, barracks and government buildings. In 2020 (again the year 20!), The whole world is now living the nightmare of the Corona Virus pandemic.

Other such chaotic epidemics claimed the lives of millions of people and whose effects on some continents were seismic. Smallpox has killed nearly 90% of the indigenous population of the United States and Latin America. It also claimed the lives of around 56 million people during the 19th century. Likewise the Cholera epidemic appeared in India, and spread to most parts of the country, then to neighboring regions, and killed a million people between 1817 and 1923. The World Health Organization described Cholera, which has infected between one and four million people a year, as a « forgotten epidemic ».

All of this has persisted into the 20th century and into our time if we shift our focus on the whole world. The Asian flu, which spread to China in 1956, and the virus that caused the H2N2 infection, was subsequently transmitted to Singapore in 1957. The resulting total number of deaths is over a million people. Then the first AIDS patient was discovered in 1981 and thousands of people around the world are still living with it reached.

Since that date, the disease has claimed the lives of 25 to 35 million people.

The cholera epidemic continues to this day, especially in Yemen where around 3,000 children died between 2016 and 2020. Another equally deadly epidemic is the swine flu which appeared in 2009 in the United States and Mexico, from where it traveled to every country in the world and resulted in the death of 18,500 people, forcing the World Health Organization to lift the state of emergency in 2010. Finally, the virus Ebola, first appeared in a small village in Guinea in 2014, then spread to a number of neighboring countries in Africa and elsewhere in the world. It killed more than 11,000 people between 2014 and 2016.

These pandemics, however, marked forms of interdependence between societies[3]. The most positive are the international cooperation they have generated. The most negative relate to the context of colonialism and what is referred to as « European expansion »[4]. In fact the « bubonic plague » which ravaged Europe caused the death of a considerable number of the peasants. The labor shortage prompted landowners to find other, much more modern means to replace traditional methods in agricultural work. This not only contributed to the development of agriculture at the time, but also contributed to the development of the European economy and prompted the « expansion of European colonialism »[5] in Africa. This expansion caused human catastrophes since it led to diseases carried by the colonizers (smallpox, measles, influenza, bubonic, malaria, diphtheria, typhus

[3] The spread of the virus contributed to the cessation of commercial activities and the weakening of the Byzantine Empire, which allowed other civilizations to reclaim land in the Middle East and North Africa and parts of it 'Asia.

[4] « Coronavirus : cinq épidémies qui ont contribué à changer le cours de l'histoire », URL: https://www.bbc.com/afrique/monde-52076467

[5] Ibid.

and cho-lera). Epidemics also have consequences on the flow and mobility of populations. African rinderpest, which spread in the late 19th century, affected animals and destroyed 90% of African livestock. Besides animal loss, it developed famine and the flight of the natives to other areas to escape the epidemic. This disaster encouraged European countries to colonize African territories abandoned by indigenous people. In fact, the epidemic may have benefited the settlers to take over land more easily. And following the famine that affected a third of Ethiopia's population, Italy seized the opportunity to invade Eritrea in the early 1890[6].

Throughout its history, Tunisia has known the spread of epidemics, in particular the plague and the cholera, which have ravaged the country and caused terrible loss of life. These two epidemics were the most devastating there for two centuries.

The scale of the plague epidemic lasting 17 months in 1784 and 1785 claimed the lives of a third of the Tunisian population. In 1785, the plague spread to the northwest and the capital, which recorded a death rate of between 200 and 250 cases per day in January and February 1785. The epidemic continued to sweep the country in the spring of the same year to reach an average of 500 deaths per day. Back home, between 1818 and 1820, the plague claimed the lives of 30,000 people in Tunis, almost a quarter of the city's population. It was considered at the time to be one of the greatest human disasters in the history of Tunisia. Subsequently, at the end of 1849, cholera spread to the region of Beja (North West), and caused hundreds of deaths in the city, people fled to the countryside to escape the epidemic which still claimed victims in 1850 in Tunis, where deaths were estimated at a hundred per day. During this period, the Bey had to isolate

---

[6] Ibid.

himself in Carthage and then in the Mohamedia Palace, and groups of the Jewish community fled to Algeria and France. The epidemic continued into spring and then into early summer, ending in August 1850.

2. CORONAVIRUS, A SOCIAL PHENOMENON

Many sociologists warn against a coronavirus which could put a damper on ailments and exchanges between inhabitants in the years to come. Measures to prevent the spread of the virus, including banning physical contact, could change human behavior. Increased awareness of infection after an outbreak could build a new generation known as « Covid-19 » refusing physical greetings or practicing social distancing to excess. Experts say the handshake's social interaction can be replaced by a remote greeting. Concerns about the maintenance of disinfectant surfaces can lead to compulsive hand cleaning behavior and persistent sales of disinfectants. From now on, the longer these procedures last, the more they will engender habits that are difficult to eliminate. If this continues, long-term changes can increase obsessive hygiene. And all of this with irreversible results.

The effect of the coronavirus on a person's psychological makeup manifests itself in contacts that have become much more virtual. It is clear that the lack of physical contact can have emotional effects for people. People are forced to work remotely and communicate through video chats, phone calls, using Skype, and hosting virtual business meetings. Increased use of technology can have long-term effects on relationships, social relations, sociability, mass communication, and exchanges.

From solidarity to behavioral changes in society

Many countries, despite their political differences, have embarked on a process of cooperation to prevent the spread of the epidemic. We see in this ordeal a solidarity that unites groups of individuals in all countries of the world. All people are equal before the Coronavirus, far from any political account. The correct management of the epidemic should only be collective and from a humanitarian point of view, because this danger does not threaten one person or another and no nation without another. In this sense, this crisis has made it possible to renew social ties. For example, many initiatives have appeared in favor of destitute elderly people: a large number of young people (girls and boys) are involved in home delivery of food and medicines, with the contribution of charitable organizations in particular. We have seen family relationships strengthened by the confinement of young people to their parents' homes, parents (caregivers in particular) forced to isolate themselves in the evening after returning from work, to protect their young children or their older elders vulnerable. We have seen the creativity of young people and artists producing concerts or music at home or on the Internet, we have also seen the change in sports practices recreated in apartments, fewer cars circulating and a nature regaining its rights over the city. We have also seen a decrease in stress and daily pressure at work, to learn to reorganize one's life between telework and family, to exercise one's profession on professional platforms, then individuals embarking on apprenticeship foreign languages.

According to studies of societal behavior, the spread of epidemics causes changes under the influence of anxiety, fear of mass death and the suffering that many people with low purchasing power endure due to unemployment, poverty and lack of medicine. It should also be noted that the imposed quarantine has resurfaced the development of domestic violence due to family proximity and confinement in homes. Imposed by most countries of the world, it has shown the disparities between poor countries and rich countries. In the absence of government aid in some countries such as Tunisia, Egypt, Morocco, Yemen and Iraq, with the exception of humanitarian aid from charitable institutions, people are seeking to work to feed their children regardless of the severity of the epidemic.

For their part, Frank Snowden in *Epidemics and Society* [7] and Stephen Taylor in *The Psychology of Epidemics*[8], explain how infectious epidemics have been able to shape society, both in the medical and health fields, as well as in the cultural, artistic and religious fields. Similarly, the neuropsychiatrist Boris Cyrulnik recalled in an interview given to Ali Rebeihi in the program Grand bien, March 16, 2020 that « with each epidemic, or natural disaster, there has been cultural change », and so it is that « our societies can withstand this crisis and become resilient ». And he goes on to show the change in European values at the time of epidemics, leading to the transition to a society discovering the arts of the house and paid work : « After the trauma, we are forced to discover new rules, new ways to live together. In the Middle Ages, we did not understand that containment had to be put in place: infected people fled, taking the bacillus with them. And in Europe, two years after the plague epidemic of 1348, one in two Europeans had disappeared. When the epidemic stopped, social values had completely changed. We had discovered the arts of the house. Previously art was

---

[7] Frank M. Snowden, *Epidemics and Society: From the Black Death to the Present*, Yale University Press, 2019. URL : https://yalebooks.yale.edu/book/9780300192216/epidemics-and-society

[8] Stephen Taylor, *The Psychology of Pandemics: Preparing for the Next Global Outbreak of Infectious Disease*, Cambridge Scholars Publishing, 2019.

predominantly religious. We saw the game and delicately painted fruits appear, the rugs under the tables. Above all, we have seen that the relations of production had changed completely : before the epidemic, most men were considered serfs and were sold with the land. After that, there were so many deaths that the survivors who agreed to work were no longer serfs: they had to be paid to make them want to work well. The relations of production and the hierarchy of values had been completely transformed »[9].

For his part, the French sociologist Alain Touraine developed the concept of a post-industrial society and worked on social movements, which he calls in France the second left with a social, democratic and social character democratic and anti-tyrannical. According to him, due to the crisis of the spread of the Covid 19 epidemic, « it is perhaps the same feeling that prevailed during the economic crisis of 1929 when everything disappeared, and that there was no actor on the scene, neither on the left nor within the governments, but Hitler quickly filled the void ». Touraine explains that this vacuum at the time is similar to that caused by the Coronavirus since its spread around the world. He notices an absence. « What surprises me today, as a contemporary sociologist or historian, is that for so long I have not felt a void that prevailed in 1929 as today. In fact, there is the absence of actors, the absence of meaning, the absence of ideas, and even of interest. We have no borders. Time is a cure or a vaccine. We don't have any weapons. Our hands are empty. We are locked up and isolated. Abandoned. We must not contact each other and above all we must get involved at home ». « We are in a vacuum. We do not

[9] « Boris Cyrulnik : Après le coronavirus, il y aura des changements profonds, c'est la règle », published by France Inter on March 16, 2020.
URL: https://www.franceinter.fr/vie-quotidienne/boris-cyrulnik-apres-le-coronavirus-il-y-aura-des-changements-profonds-c-est-la-regle

speak and we must not act, but more than that, we do not understand what is going on »[10]. Alain Touraine estimated that the Corona pandemic will be followed by major ecological disasters over the next ten years, and will lead to an economic shock capable of producing political reactions which he classified as fascist. This vacuum can have huge effects on social and political stability and on the world economy, he says, or cause the collapse of entire societies and nations. It can seriously prelude to a rise in dictatorships within so-called democratic regimes.

The management of the crisis by the Tunisian authorities

New practices were deployed during the confinement period in order to make life easier for the most vulnerable people and in order to re-establish links both with our loved ones and within the framework of teleworking. However, teleworking is more suited to some countries than others. Although digital technology has brought important professional changes to Tunisia, shortages persist.

For its part, the Tunisian government wanted to support a reorganization of work based on digital platforms in companies or at the university. However, even if higher education has distinguished itself in recent years by distance learning, the question is whether everyone (students and teachers) can adapt to this system. Are students able to take the courses remotely ? Do they have the necessary logistical means (computers and internet connection) ?

It should also be seen that distance education, a newly established educational method, relies, among other

---

[10] « Cette crise du Covid-19 va pousser les soignants vers le haut », Alain Touraine, sociologue au journal « El País », 7 avril 2020.
URL: http://www.espaces-latinos.org/archives/90174

things, on the provision of a specific educational program that challenges the traditional teaching conditions of universities. The idea of distance education emerged in the late 1970s in American and European universities. This method consisted of sending recordings and teaching programs to all students by mail, in order to provide a full explanation of the content of the subjects programmed in their university course. Students merged the two learning methods and followed all assigned instructions. The exams were then taken on the university campus at the end of the year.

One of the disadvantages of distance education is that of working long, continuous and continuous hours, which interferes with personal life and makes the person vulnerable to mental and physical stress. Likewise, the high cost of the equipment and training required for this type of education is noted. In addition, the opportunities of this method in terms of employment, productivity and equal opportunities are not always well understood in ministries and especially in Arab countries. Nonetheless, distance education plays a major role in improving the cultural, scientific and social norms of individuals. It helps to fill the shortage of qualified teachers in various fields, and facilitates access to educational resources for teachers as well as students and pupils. As such, it provides comprehensive and innovative thematic and logistical support to training institutions and teaching techniques, and decreases the use of intermediaries.

The crisis in Tunisia has given rise to numerous public and financial failures, and considerably exacerbated the medical sector. Despite the professionalism of the staff in place, we can say that the lack of equipment and the fragility of the workforce of its medical framework, constitute a crucial issue. This has been exacerbated by the emigration of a large number of Tunisian doctors in recent years, as well as by the policy of stopping public service secondments as part of the commitment of successive governments to implement an austerity policy contained in the conditions dictated by the International Monetary Fund during the extension of the extended loan in 2016. To this is added a budgetary crisis in the health sector, which saw its share of public spending total decreases in recent years. It is true that far fewer cases than in Europe and China were proportionally recorded in Tunisia during the spring of 2020. But the rate of confirmed infections has greatly increased thereafter, and Tunisia could face a disaster unable to fight because of the fragility of its health system. Public hospitals suffer from a lack of basic and specialty equipment, as well as a lack of adequate supplies (drugs, health equipment and devices, protective masks, respirators, etc.). Note only 300 resuscitation beds available to patients, a very low figure to cope with the pandemic.

This health system is on the verge of collapsing despite the efforts of the state and civil society. In this sense, several controversies have arisen as to the veracity of the figures officially given, without response to date, on the management of the pandemic (sterilization, sanitation of public places, cleanliness of common areas, observation on the behavior of citizens, exhortation to respect social isolation in addition to the strict application of the quarantine). As such and in the face of this lack of information, rumors and Fakenews have exploded. Among other counter-announcements on supposed figures and events but inciting a spirit of criticism and analysis, digital networks have launched a multitude of information according to which a Tunisian researcher working in Germany has discovered a vaccine against the corona virus, Dr Radwan Kamoun. Some sites have even mentioned hypothetical contacts between this doctor and the Tunisian and then American presidents ! In fact, some Tunisian scientists residing in Germany, have questioned the authenticity of the message and the circulating information, considering that Dr Radwan Kamoun is a real person and seems to be successful in his field of work, but it is possible that his name was « used in a fraud ». Similar information has circulated about a certain photochemist professor Mahmoud Abdelkader Benzarti assassinated on April 3, 2020 in Germany, who is said to have been about to conclude the discovery of the vaccine against the coronavirus.

In March 2020, the Tunisian government took the same restrictive measures applied in China and Europe, proactive and publicized, in order to limit the spread of the epidemic. This first management of the epidemic was relatively reasonable and swift. Immediately after the announcement of the first patient with a positive test result in early March 2020, airport and port authorities began to take temperature measurements for travelers arriving in the country, and to impose a quarantine on those from the European Union. Then the government tightened its precautionary measures with remarkable speed and, over the next two weeks, imposed further restrictions to stop work in the country. Home confinement has been in place since March 22 with a night curfew throughout the country from 6 p.m. to 6 a.m. Public life has ceased after the closure of schools, universities, cafes, restaurants, mosques, certain industries, the stoppage of public transport, and restrictions on travel between and within cities. The establishments related to health, energy, communications, and the production of food and cleaning products have escaped these measures. However, by what means have the authorities reacted to the transgressors of the confinement ?

Strict decisions have been taken against the violation of mandatory quarantine by some citizens. The government held a ministerial meeting on April 13, during which it issued a statement containing a package of measures to limit the spread of the coronavirus in the country. It was decided to develop a national program to preserve overall health throughout the country. By imposing a global quarantine, the state addressed the general epidemiological situation, and imposed severe provisions on violators of the curfew and quarantine rules. These measures may have had counterproductive effects as they prompted hundreds of citizens to stand in front of post offices, especially retirees, needy families and the poor, in addition to the large number of people outside the shops food, which was likely to promote contagion.

For the application of the global quarantaine and the curfew, the Tunisian State relied on article 50 of 1978 concerning the regulation of the state of emergency, which confers on the Minister of the Interior (in its chapters 4-5-6) exceptional powers which include the prohibition of the movement of people and vehicles without prior legal authorization, the prevention of gatherings, the closing of shops, cafes, mosques. However, the punishment of quarantine offenders is régie by Law No. 92 of 1992 in Chapter 18, which states that « anyone who willfully conducts his behavior will be punished with imprisonment. Anyone who leaves the hospital to which he has been admitted is obliged, even for a short time, to apply Chapter 19 of the law ». In both cases, the sentence is imposed in a hospital prison. Likewise, a decree was issued, allowing a financial penalty of 50 dinars to be imposed in the event that the quarantine measures are not respected. Nonetheless, unacceptable abuses of power were committed during this period. Some citizens have been harassed when they have to work in areas permitted by law while in lockdown. The digital networks cited as such the physical police assault of a young delivery man at home who, following his complaint, found himself the subject of a police report accusing him of being to spread false news that affects public order. Even the collection of donations for the benefit of poor families by young volunteers in different parts of the country has not been spared the harassment of security agents. The most remarkable case is that of the arrest of the head of the organization I Wake Up, Achraf Awadi collecting donations of medicines for the hospital of Djerba, arrested at the Bouchoucha detention center for violation of the curfew while he supported the national effort to prevent the pandemic. Police suspicion also arises when requesting permission for photographs in places not required for licensing. We can also cite this fact of the district of La Goulette where the security forces arrested the young student, Mohamed Amin Saadou after he posted a video clip on Facebook, in which he spoke of the uselessness of the sterilization equipment used by the municipality of La Goulette. The blogger's two-day arrest in Bouchoucha left him vulnerable to transmission of the infection, especially since the detention center does not meet the minimum requirements for safety and human dignity.

3. ECONOMIC CRISIS AND SPECULATIONS DURING A PERIOD OF CONFINEMENT, FROM ALGERIA TO MOROCCO AND TUNISIA

Fraudsters at various levels often seek to exploit crises to enrich themselves through speculation, black markets, fraud and rumors. Following the imposed lockdown, the epidemic was no exception in some countries, prompting authorities to take action to deal with those they have compared to « war criminals ».

In Algeria, during the month of April, 44 million Algerians faced a serious shortage of se-mold (wheat flour) after massive purchases of this staple food caused by a rumor of exhaustion of stocks, widely transmitted by Facebookers. Algerian President Abdelmajid Tebboune tried to reassure citizens by telling them that the stock of semolina was sufficient to meet demand for four or five months, and he called for denouncing the monopolists. However, this did not alleviate the pressure on the outlets of the mills, where crowds gathered daily to obtain a sack of semolina at the subsidized price. This prompted the Ministry of Commerce, because of the risk of transmission of the virus, to announce the ban on these gatherings.

Between March 22 and April 1, the national gendarmerie and the Algerian police arrested more than 2,500 people who were stocking basic food and pharmaceutical products for monopoly and speculation purposes. During this period, more than five thousand tons of food were seized and around 219,000 pharmaceutical items. In this Maghreb country at the outset most affected by the epidemic, the Internet has become the means of transmitting misleading information which maintains confusion and the spread of rumors about the imminent closure of gas stations, caused by traffic jams and congestion in most Algerian cities, while the procedure only concerned the city of Blida, near Algiers, and the first epicenter of the epidemic. These rumors were arrested by the « online investigators » of the Algerian gendarmerie. Others have sounded alerts. Like this Oranaise who published a video clip denouncing citizens in quarantine in a tourist resort in the region, after their return from abroad, for having escaped their period of confinement using their influences. Or the director and editor-in-chief of the newspaper « The Other Voice », which had published an article on probable errors during medical examinations to detect people suffering from the Corona virus.

Unfortunately, as is the case in Morocco and Tunisia, death is counted in the thousands in Algeria. It seems that this has started an economic crisis, due to the damage caused by the virus. With oil prices having fallen below the $ 30 mark, the Algerian budget, generally based on the price of a barrel above $ 50, will not be able to absorb the drop in income as the crisis unfolds continues to this day. Algeria's losses have been estimated, according to unofficial estimates, at around $ 1 billion per month (during the period February 1 to March 30, 2020), due to the drop in the price of a barrel. It should be noted that Algeria depends, in its income from hard currencies, 98% of its oil and gas exports, 50% of oil taxation, and 70% of salaries are paid on the basis of these revenues. Algeria deals more with the European Union, and in particular with Italy and Spain (connection by gas pipelines), which in this first period are the most affected by the Corona virus crisis, and at risk of interruption or suspension of payments.

Likewise if the crisis continues, the tax on oil which was expected at 2800 billion Algerian dinars will be reduced by half, which means an additional deficit of 1.4 trillion dinars in addition to the expected initial deficit of 1.5 trillion dinars : deficit which will double to reach the value of 2800 billion Algerian dinars. The Algerian government would then have to enter into a choice between two options, either resorting to unconventional financing by printing money, a step that the penultimate government had taken previously and which has attracted much criticism, or rely on external financing through loans that remain on its part, a red line that Algeria rejects.

With regard to Morocco [11] , March 19, 2020, the Moroccan government declared the state of emergency sanitation, and restricted travel in the country, after having previously decided to suspend all theft. Friday, April 17 In

[11] Morocco is a developing country, with an economy dedicated to the market, with a strong presence of the public authorities in investment and in the orientation of economic policies. Morocco is the fifth economic power in Africa, after Egypt, Nigeria, Algeria and South Africa, with a GDP estimated at 104 billion dollars (235.14 billion taking into account the parity of the powers purchase), averaging $ 3,108 per person.

the evening, the total number of victims of the Corona virus in Morocco has increased to 135 deaths and 2,150 cases, after the first case recorded on March 2nd. Since the beginning of the registration of cases of coronavirus in Morocco, the General Union of Marocan markets (the largest gathering of companies in the country called « Al Batrona »), proposed a set of measures to mitigate the negative impact of the propagation of the vir At the same time on March 17, the government decided to create a $ 1 billion funded fund, to "cover expenditures related to the rehabilitation of mechanisms and health », as well as to keep pace with the most affected sectors such as tourism. For its part, speculation began on the products in high demand during the quarantine period. The speculators rushed to buy all the masks even those used in protection in the chantrees ! And prices for alcoholic solutions have increased.

In the city of Fez (North), the police arrested four people suspected of leading a "secret workshop" in a garage for the manufacture and marketing of disinfectors. In another case, people have plagiarized the status of state agents participating in salé health awareness campaigns near Rabat, and commis a number of flights. In the same context, the United Nations Development Program in Rabat warned at the end of March 2020, some of the region who claim to be part of UNDP staff and lead fraudulent activities.

Economically, Moroccan tourism is one of the sectors most affected by the pandemic. The majority of tourist activities have been canceled, and the flights to destination or from Morocco suspended, with strong business benefits. The Kingdom already loses 6 million tourists the first months of this year 2020, a great loss of currency for this sector based on Europe.

The tourism sector in Morocco provides 750,000 emplois, and it represents 7% of the gross domestic product. He had revenue from 78.6 billion dirhams (8.25 million dollars) in 2019, up 7.7% compared to 2018.

In Tunisia also, the authorities tightened the con- state of speculators and monopolies At the end of March, Customs seized gloves, suspicious suits and masks for a value of 500,000 dinarsTunisian (158,000 euros) in the port of Radès, near the capital, in the warehouse of a The President of the Republic called upon to follow the speculators he qualified as « Criminels of war » after exhausted stocks of flour and semolina in some areas. Still in Tunisia, a state official, who works with the Kef Governorate (North West) was arrested in the Kef City, after having been denounced by the Native Anti-Corruption Commission, which has accused many employees to be involved. It is a secret to person than billion dollar money circulates coming from and from Libya and Algeria, especially with the Algerian border. It is a secret for permission that foreign currency exchanges are made in the foreign exchange market in the capital of Tunis and in particular to « Bab Bahr » near Tunis souks, no one checks if these exchange rates comply with the official rates. These operations are under the gaze of security agents, and there is no more secret for anyone than currency traders and money laundering speculate through the border without going through the Tunisian office. These speculators have allies, or even « militias » that monopolize the black market in all the departments of the governorate and the Ministry of the Interior and the Ministry of Finance.

The demand for foreign currency is growing in tunisia due to inflation and political crisis. The purchase of the euro to cover each other has become one of the crises that hit the Tunisian Dinar. These corruption practices have even been mentioned by the President of the Republic in one of his speeches to the National Security Council, of April 1, stating that « in 2012, the Tunisian public treasury was looted by 10,000 to 13,500 thousand million Liards of dinars ». He later traveled to Algeria to borrow $ 150 million to deposit at the Central Bank of Tunisia.

Today in Tunisia, and despite a half and very favorable drop in oil prices, the crisis, marked by strong dependence on European economies, is affecting the various sectors of the economy. national economy: forecast for a decrease of 21% in the tourism sector, 30% in the air sector and 50% in the maritime transport sector. In this respect, it should be noted that France, Germany and Italy represent the main market for Tunisian tourism. Note also that Tunisian exports fell sharply to the euro zone.

Regarding the financial aid provided by the West to the countries of the southern Mediterranean to control the epidemic, it seems that Algeria did not benefit from it, and that two payments were made in spring 2020, in Tunisia and Morocco, the first for 300 million euros (968.416.560 dinars) and the second for 150 million euros (484.208.280 dinars) by the European Anti-Proliferation Fund of Corona. At the same time, the Ambassador of the European Union in Tunisia, Patrice Bergamini, said that the EU will continue to support the « Aziz » program for the rehabilitation of health services by doubling the aid allocated by 20 million euros for the benefit of 13 regions, or 60 million euros for all Tunisian governorates. It is certain that this financial assistance will not reach all the Tunisian regions, and that a large part of the sums allocated will be used for other ends and for speculative purposes.

4. FINANCES AND AN ECONOMY UNDER INTERNATIONAL DEPENDANCE

Since the era of the Troika, the inflation rate has increased rapidly in Tunisia, after reaching 7.8% in June 2020, it rose at the end of the year to 8.4%, while prices continue to rise and the exchange rate of the local currency decreases, which will affect the purchasing power of Tunisians. In this sense, we note a strong marginalization of the financial question by the various State actors, which results in lack of strategy or the ambiguity of the recommended solutions. Added to this is an unprecedented increase in public spending and little attention paid to investment and exports. In this problematic context, the Tunisian government has still not taken effective measures to consolidate its budget, in particular to increase the tax revenues of certain taxpayers who have so far been spared, and to curb salary increases.

For its part, the Tunisian banking system has submitted to economic liberalization over the years. For several years, Islamic finance from the Near and Middle East has been booming there. « Islamic finance is now an important part of the development programs of the countries of the Middle East and North Africa (MENA), and it is also gaining ground in the financial landscape of the region. This is a booming activity, which responds to the financial needs of individuals in respect for their social and religious values »[12]. Take the example of the Islamic bank Zitouna, seized by Sakhr Matri, son-in-law of the former president of the Tunisian republic Ben Ali, who held 87% of its capital. This bank was under the supervision of the Rotschild business network but was confiscated by the state after the fall of the former president. His ambition was to make Tunisia the financial center of North Africa and to improve Islamic services.

In fact, the banking system, whatever it is, does not serve the interests of individuals. Rather, it promotes the advantages of bankers and lenders. The international banking system today, despite the intentions expressed by development programs (from the World Bank to the International Monetary Fund), perpetuates poverty in the

[12] Salman Syed Ali, « Islamic banking in the Middle-East and North-Africa (MENA) Region », Islamic Economic Studies, Vol. 20, n ° 1, 2012

world, as banks seek to increase their profits through loans granted. We will take the case of microfinance institutions which belong to the large international banks and which finance the projects of the poorest in the world. It has been shown in this sense that this access to consumer finance is part of a spiral of small indebtedness among beneficiaries in the face of the multiplicity of funding organizations (one borrows from another in order to be able to repay previous loans). This is about solidarity displayed by big business, and not about cooperation between government institutions and civil society[13].

Tunisia does not have its own products, in other words it is only free to manage its national resources (wheat, olives, oil, etc.) with the approval and dependence of international finance. For example : In 2019, the Tunisian durum wheat harvest brought 35 million quintals. Part of this harvest, about 15.000 quintals, was abandoned due to weak state demand for national redistribution, lack of space in storage areas, and washed away by the rain. Thus official figures show, despite the record harvest in summer 2019, a sharp increase in grain imports from abroad. Tunisia imported 514,000 tonnes of durum wheat at the end of October at a cost of 442 million Tunisian dinars, 462.000 tonnes of barley for 322 million dinars and 1.081.000 tonnes of soft wheat at 734 million dinars. As a result, Tunisian wheat, sold in dollars, is a valuable and quality commodity that is exported to Western countries. In return and despite its good production, Tunisia imports wheat and barley from the USA. In addition to all these imports, Tunisia imported 35% of its milling wheat needs and 50% of its barley needs from France.

---

[13] Houda Laroussi, *Micro-crédit et lien social. La solidarité instituée*, Karthala, Paris, 2009 ; Houda Laroussi, *Femmes et développement local en Tunisie. Acteurs et enjeux*, L'Harmattan, Paris, 2018.

SECOND PART

Geopolitics of the new international order

For the West and the countries of the Arab world, the revolution that began in Tunisia was unexpected. Many commentators today see it as chaos that strayed from its original goals. What really happened, who are the actors involved and the international strategies, often overlooked, and what has happened since ?

1. THE ARAB UPRISES

The Arab revolutions, or the Arab winter revolutions, are imposing movements, often peaceful, which began in certain Arab countries in late 2010 and early 2011, affected by the Tunisian revolution which erupted after the "sacrifice" of Mohamed Bouazizi to protest against the deterioration of his living conditions and his inability to provide the means of subsistence to his family. The revolution started with unprecedented popular uprisings, spread across the country, then subsided on January 14, when Zine El Abidine Ben Ali flew for Jeddah in Arabia Arabia. The country was plagued by dictatorship, political corruption, social restrictions and injustices, unemployment and the jobs crisis.

Eleven days later, the Egyptian revolution of January 25 broke out, followed by the Yemeni revolution, and on

February 11, Muhammad Hosni Mubarak announced his resignation, was jailed after trying to kill demonstrators during the riots. After the overthrow of these two Tunisian and Egyptian regimes, peaceful protests began to call for an end to corruption and an improvement in living conditions, which subsequently spread to other parts of the Arab world.

We can cite the Libyan revolution of February 17 with the assassination of Muammar Gaddafi and the overthrow of his regime, the Yemeni revolution which forced Ali Ab¬doullah Saleh to resign, then the Sudanese revolution of 2019 which overthrew the former President Omar El-Bashir. These movements and others enshrined the outbreak of civil wars - Lybie, Yemen, Syria, Iraq - as well as the rise of the Islamic State (Iraq), and reached all parts of the Arab world. These revolutions were marked by the emergence of the slogan that first appeared in Tunisia and became popular in all Arab countries : « The people want to overthrow the regime ».

We have noted since the modification of the Moroccan constitution in 2011, the coup d'état of July 3, 2013 which ousted President Mohamed Morsi from power in Egypt, then the abolition of the 2012 constitution adopted under his influence and replaced in 2014, as well as the new Tunisian constitution of 2014. Note that the latter has among others called to try to end the Palestinian division between Fatah and Hamas and many other countries. Why these events and what reasons are at the origin: a high proportion of citizens living below the poverty line, ignorance and illiteracy affecting an entire population, the constant rise in prices, the increase in unemployment, repression and tyranny, political corruption of leaders, asserted violations of human rights.What objectives have motivated them : Achieve a decent life for the citizen; overthrow the corrupt system ; call for a national dialogue ; establish a democratic system.

2. THE COLLAPSE OF GLOBAL TRADE

The International Monetary Fund expects this year 2020 to have an economic recession worse than that experienced by Western countries during the 2008 global crisis. Memory takes us back to Tuesday, October 29, 1929, called Black Tuesday, after its collapse Previous 5 days ago on Thursday October 24, 1929, as the first stage of the world economic crisis of the 1930s of the 20th century known as the Great Depression. This is due to an incredibly higher supply than demand, as almost 19 million shares were offered on the sell list, which brought the price of each to its lowest level.

All economic sectors were affected by the crisis, as well as the labor market, leading to massive layoffs. According to Le Monde newspaper of May 08, 2020, « The unemployment rate in the United States has never been higher since the Great Depression. In two months, the health and economic crisis destroyed more than 33 million jobs, pushing the unemployment rate to a level worthy of the crisis of the 1930s »[14]. This rise in unemployment led to massive layoffs following the closure of a large number of businesses but also the loss of jobs in several sectors related to hotels, restaurants, large industries, logistics, etc.

The international labor organization, for its part, has sounded the alarm over the impact of the crisis caused by the epidemic on the labor market. She said 25 million jobs were threatened by the crisis and there could be more than 40 million. The epidemic could « destroy between 5.3 million and 24.7 million jobs worldwide. This compared to the base figure of 188 million in 2019. The pessimistic scenario would thus be higher than the number of

[14] URL: https://www.lemonde.fr/economie/article/2020/05/08/aux-etats-unis-le-taux-de-chomage-au-plus-haut-depuis-50-ans_6039101_3234.html.

unemployed provoked by the 2008-2009 crisis (22 million people) »[15].

At the end of the first half of 2020, we are living one of the great moments in history with the collapse of the world stock markets, the price of the dollar, foreign and Arab currencies, the confirmed bankruptcy of many companies, the layoffs thousands of workers, losses already in the order of $ 7.5 trillion. Note that the 100 richest people in the world lost about $ 444 billion in just two months. In this sense, Bill Gates and Bernard Arnault, the richest, come in second, with a loss of 10 billion dollars after Jeff Bezos, founder of the company Amazon, whose wealth has fallen to 11.9 billion dollars. Likewise, the Gulf stock markets suffered losses of 76 billion dollars and as a result industrial activity lost 30% of its values.

Global debt continues to grow, and the US monetary deficit is expected to reach $ 3.8 trillion, which represents 18.7% of the output of the US economy. In the Arab world, the loss has reached 25%, and up to 27% in the Gulf countries. Deficits in Saudi Arabia have risen to 2 trillion, oil prices have fallen by around 20%, and losses in Tunisia are estimated at 60 billion dinars in the hospitality sector. In this case, losses in the sports sector all over the world are in the order of 40%, approximately $ 4 trillion.

As for global markets, in March 2020 stock indices in Britain and Germany fell around 7%, the general index fell 5% in Japan and 7% in Australia. The Chinese market in Shanghai fell 3%, while the Arab markets saw variable declines, especially in Saudi Arabia, where the overall index fell more than 9%. For their part, the main US stock indexes lost more than 20% in the spring of 2020. The

[15] Tribune, « Coronavirus : la crise pourrait mettre au chômage 25 millions de personnes dans le monde », 18 mars 2020.
URL: https://www.latribune.fr/economie/international/coronavirus-la-crise-pourrait-mettre-to-unemployment-25-million-people-in-the-world-842616.html

world gold market has also been affected, but in a different way, especially in the Gulf countries and East Asia.

In fact, the relationship between the virus and gold is direct. The higher the index of « victims », the higher the price of gold due to the desire of those seeking refuge to buy it from other investments such as the financial and oil markets. In this sense at the end of March 2020 the price of gold recorded an increase coinciding with the spread of the Coronavirus, which prompted investors to buy safe assets, while futures contracts on US gold rose. 0.2%. Finally, « victim n ° 1 » is oil, of which China is the world's largest importer and consumer. For example, on Thursday, March 26, 2020, Brent Crude fell to $ 55.71 per barrel, while West Texas Intermediate was at $ 51.24 per barrel.

3. THE USA, REGULATORS OF THE WORLD ORDER

The corona virus pandemic has given rise to multiple interpretations around the international geopolitical situation. The crisis is now situated in a globalized and interdependent context, where the strategies of the great powers are organizing a new order and new orientations for the conduct of the world. These, if we look at history, have gone through a number of crises producing important changes on an international scale. Wars waged by colonial states, for example, were the means to appropriate and exploit indigenous wealth.

Interference in world affairs

During his speech at the Texas Academy of Sciences in 2006, environmentalist Pianka said the Ebola virus would be a solution to the overpopulation problem ». He adds that « humanity must be reduced to 500 million inhabitants »[16], and that this is part of the « new world economic order ». Likewise Henry Kissinger has declared that limiting the world's population is a national security objective of the United States : « You can control the five continents and by controlling food and agriculture, you control the world population »[17]. In an announced 1979 speech, former US Secretary of Defense Robert McNamara said that the increase in the world's population was the biggest problem and the greatest disaster for the economic and social development of the country world : « we therefore have from this moment and not tomorrow to prevent the world population from reaching ten billion people ». He then spoke of the two methods of achieving this, either reducing the birth rate or increasing the death rate. In the latter case, besides famine and disease, bacterial or nuclear wars were suggested.

It will be remembered here that the colonizer was already allocating the natural resources of the occupied peoples for his own benefit, and that the numerous famines or epidemics decimating the populations could constitute increased opportunities to establish themselves. As such, we will give the example of the British establishment in India. Economist B.M. Bhatia explains in his book *Famines in India*[18], that after the advent of British colonialism, from 1859 to 1914, the country began to witness a major famine almost every two years. As the rest of the world witnessed an increase in population due to technological advancements, the population remained

[16] David Jarry, « Dr. Eric Pianka Told University of Texas in 2006: Use of Ebola Would Exterminate 90% of the World's Population », published October 1, 2014, Webmaster.
URL: http://conscience-du-peuple.blogspot.com/2012/01/le-scientifique-dr-eric-r-pianka-defend.html

[17] Henry Kissinger, *L'ordre du monde*, Fayard, Paris, 2016.

[18] B.M. Bhatia, *Famines in India : a study in some aspects of the economic history of India*, 1860-1945, Asia Publishing House, 1963.

stable for nearly a century, as the famine situation was the mainstay of colonial strategy in India. It would seem today, that « the new world economic order » driven by the United States and based on the appropriation of indigenous wealth, is organized around loans granted to poor countries to keep them alive even when they are ravaged by famines and pests. Nowadays the corona virus is entering a new world order. What will be its impact and its spin-offs ?

For more than a century, the United States has interfered in the affairs of many countries of the world, including the South American continent, directly or indirectly, including supporting numerous coups d'état. Washington's first intervention in Latin America dates back to 1898, when Puerto Rico and Cuba, which were under Spanish colonial rule, were occupied. The occupation ended in 1902, but its influence continued for years. Four years later, the United States overthrew Cuba's first elected president, Thomas Estrada Palma, and formed an occupying government that ruled the country until 1909. In 1917, after having occupied Haiti, the United States reoccupied Cuba and gradually began to withdraw from it in 1923. The United States also wanted to control the project of the Panama Canal left by the French and against Colombia, supported the separatist forces and Panamanian terrorism. They subsequently retained their influence there and waged a diplomatic and economic war there until 1989. They also occupied Nicaragua until 1933, which they then supported as well as in Honduras the coups to facilitate the work of the American fruit companies in the countries of the region. They also sent armed forces to Mexico to fight the Zapatista revolution. Note also the bloody Vietnam War that began in 1955, which resulted in the death of more than 3.000.000 Vietnamese civilians, and nearly 60.000 American soldiers and more than 300.000 wounded.

Finally, the United States stood out in what they called « the war on terrorism » following the events of September 11, 2001. However, many commentators have pointed out multiple anomalies or questions in the course of the proceedings incidents. The first would have concerned the problematic discovery of the passport of Muhammad Atta, responsible for the first plane crash, amid the rubble and ash of the north tower. The second relates to the fire which devastated the tons of steel in the towers, which could only be destroyed by internal explosives on the lower floors, in a context where the anti-missile defense system should have destroyed the aggressor plane[19]. Others relate to leases of rentals and insurance or sales of shares contracted by American billionaires a few days or weeks before the attack. It would follow that this event would have largely justified the American strikes carried - against Afghanistan on November 9, 2001, and announced the start of their military operations against terrorism, then on March 20, 2003, the invasion of Iraq by coalition forces with 250.000 American soldiers and 45,000 sol - British dates. It should be noted in this regard that this occupation of Iraq killed 655,000 Iraqis, displacing millions more, and saw the deaths of more than 4.421 American soldiers.

A project for an « American military base » in the south of Tunisia

Other sources of information report in particular on digital networks that Tunisian President Béji Caid Essebsi refused to establish an American military base and a liaison office in Tunisia, in the city of Rmada, in the governorate of Medenine, the southernmost border of Tunisia, adjacent to the desert triangle from which terrorist

[19] Andreas Von Bülow, *Die CIA und der 11 septembre. Internationaler Terror und die Rolle der Geheimdienste*, Piper Verlag GmbH, Munich, 2003.

groups, in particular Al Qaeda, take a stronghold. This establishment would have been proposed by the leader of the party Ennahdha Rached Ghannouchi in Washington in 2012, after having won the elections of 2011. This desire would have been reiterated during a visit of the American Republican Senator John McCain to the leader of the Tunisian State on Friday February 6, 2015, confirming this wish to establish a military base in the south of Tunisia, following the deterioration of the security situation in Libya. This intention echoed the fall of the Gaddafi regime and the entry of armed Islamic militias into Tripoli. Its aim was to fight against terrorist groups on the borders of Libya and Algeria, because of the dangers posed by the « Fajr Libya »[20] and « Islamic State » militias on the stability of countries in the region, to later convert to the central command center of the AFRICOM force in North Africa. Essebsi saw in this a risk of affecting the sovereignty of the Tunisian state and its foreign policy. We can read in this reaction a similar attitude taken by Habib Bourguiba, founder of the independent Tunisian state, when he confided to the American ambassador in Tunisia, asking for the establishment of a military base in 1982: « the Mediterranean waters are wide and deep. They can accommodate the sixth fleet and also a military base. As for Tunisia, which has good relations with you, it is a small country, but it rejects any interference in its internal affairs by any country, even if it is the United States ». The refusal of the former head of state Caid Essebsi reflects a general position of politicians and Tunisian civil society, which would see in the American military bases, « hotbeds » used by the United States to abort any successful experiment and extend their influence to the

[20] Fajr Libya is a coalition of armed groups with an Islamist tendency during the Second Libyan Civil War, the core of which is made up of the militias of the city of Misrata, with around it a large part of the militias from the South." URL: https://fr.wikipedia.org/wiki/Fajr_Libya

region as part of a new scheme to serve their vital interests. For many Tunisians, the United States, with the help of generous quatari funding, would have played a major role by supporting, through their diplomatic relations and their communication media, the rise of the Ennahdha party in 2011, despite the condemnation by the Tunisian democratic parties deeply shocked by this support.

John McCain described Rached Ghannouchi as « the godfather of the Muslim Brotherhood ». Likewise, Hammadi Jebali, when he was at the head of the Troika government led by Ennahdha, agreed to this promise by Rached Ghannouchi in 2012.

This harmonization in relations between the two Tunisian-American officials was described by Arab and foreign diplomats in 2012 as the « honeymoon » between Ennahdha and Washington, where the head of the government Hammadi Jebali, traveled to Washington in May at the invitation of Congress, and where he met with senior White House officials and policymakers such as John McCain and Joe Lieberman, as well as Secretary of State John Kerry. During 2012, the same sources report that marine forces worked alongside Tunisian soldiers for months, and oversaw the preparation of a « US-Tunisian military base » in southern Tunisia. It was at this time that the American media, followed in this sense by European counterparts, even by certain French diplomats, carried out a strong campaign to promote the image of the Ennahdha movement as representing moderate political Islam, while Rached Ghannouchi reassured Americans that he was against the application of Sharia law and for a civil status system.

4. FROM EUROPE TO CHINA

The crisis is reshaping the structure of world power. The management of the virus will continue to put pressure on economic activities and increase tensions between countries and within themselves, to the benefit of those who have been able to resolve it to date.

The war against the Coronavirus, as French President Macron has mentioned, is the war of all states against a single enemy. Today, the handling of the Coronavirus crisis has demonstrated the failure of the United States and the West in general to rule the world as before. The balance of power in the world system is undergoing a radical change. Outside of WHO (World Health Organization), we are witnessing the failure of international institutions to play a decisive role in coordinating the various partners to manage or even reduce the crisis. The latter could ultimately lead to the disintegration of the European Union. For its part, the European Union is going through one of the strongest crises of its existence, with the exceptional closure of its borders like them were during the Cold War years and before the collapse of the Berlin Wall. This pandemic has indeed shown that most EU governments have waged a fight on their own. Each government has opted for self-sufficient and self-sufficient protectionism, which has helped cover both its hostility to immigration and its declining interest in issues of sustainable development and climate change. The Italian government, in an unstable financial situation before the crisis, has unsuccessfully asked for help from the countries of the European Union. It was finally China that offered its services to the countries affected by the epidemic (sending Chinese doctors and masks), not only to Italy but also and among others to Spain, Serbia, Algeria, Morocco, Tunisia, South Korea. Chinese planes have landed during the crisis at

European airports loaded with medicines, as if they were not affected by the epidemic. Apart from Germany, which has repatriated a few French patients to its hospitals, European cooperation is almost absent.

Now, the whole world is focused on China and the countries of Southeast Asia, and more specifically on the strategy they adopted to deal with and contain the Coronavirus crisis. The Corona virus will transform an America-centric globalization into a China-centric globalization, whose current battle over the coronavirus shows today has won the war. The United States continues to accuse China of concealing from the international community the severity of the Coronavirus as well as the exact number of victims, in order to protect its economy and confirm its leadership over the United States. And for its part, the Chinese government claims that the United States is at the origin of the Corona virus.

For his part, the President of the United States has decided, faced with the development of Chinese industry and the scale of his business, to carry out all the operations to immobilize him. These include the interventions of his economic advisor Peter Navarro [21] who led the US president to wage the trade war against China. In 2006, he published *The Next Wars for China*. His second book was released in 2011 and titled *Death by China*. Peter Navarro emphasizes the danger caused by the enormous trade imbalance between the United States and China, as well as the negative impact of this inequality on the American economy. An ardent defender of free trade and favorable to the redistribution of wealth within social groups, Peter Navarro focused his economic, social and financial studies on China's unfair trade policies after she joined the World

---

[21] Peter Navarro is an American economist. He has been appointed as Assistant to the US President in the Executive Office and the National Trade Council of the White House by Donald Trump since 20 January 2017.
URL: https://en.wikipedia.org/wiki/Death_by_China

Trade Organization in 2001. The latter event, according to Navarro, would have harmed the American and European economy, directly and indirectly, would have increased the trade deficit and caused the loss of employment of a significant number of Americans. And this is because of the large number of American companies and factories that move to China to work in a cheap, state-funded environment. With the crisis unleashed between the United States and China, the world risks finding itself in yet another war similar to the Cold War.

This is what prompted Chinese-born American banker Song Hongjing[22] to write the book *Currency War*, in which he warned China against a group of private banks allegedly taking control of state-owned banks. American. The author tells the story of a group of European bankers, under the aegis of the Rothschild family network, which would have gradually controlled the European and then American central banks. Thus says the site referred : « By mastering finance, they have directed modern history, whether during the American Civil War, the two world wars, the crisis of 1929, or the fall of the Soviet Union. . More recently, the Japanese recession of the 1990s and the Asian crisis of 1997 are also attributed to the actions of these occult bankers. According to Song, these bankers are trying to subject the economy - and especially the Chinese economy - to their diktats in order to retain financial power. He recommends that the Chinese adopt the gold standard in order to protect themselves »[23].

The great world powers have underestimated the economic, social and military strength of China, with an industry developed in all areas, especially the automotive,

---

[22] Song Hongjing, *La Guerre des monnaies. La Chine et le Nouvel Ordre mondial*, Editions Le Retour aux Sources, Paris, 2013.

[23] URL : https://fr.wikipedia.org/wiki/La_Guerre_des_monnaies._La_Chine_et_le_Nouvel_Ordre_mondial

electronics, missile industries intercontinentals. 70% of Chinese work in modern technology. It is now asserting its dominance over the United States. The war between the two powers thus manifested itself in the context of the coronavirus crisis. It started from a Tweet posted by Chinese Foreign Ministry spokesman Zhao Legan on Twitter on March 12, 2020, indicating the possibility that it was « the US military that brought the novel Corona virus (Covid-19) » in the Chinese region of Wuhan, from which it has started to spread. This tweet updated the already popular American conspiracy theory on Chinese digital networks. It suggests that 300 US military athletes competing in the Seventh World Military Games in Wuhan in October 2019 were infected with the virus and then spread to Wuhan and throughout China. According to the same sources, May 7 2020, Chinese doctor Liu was shot dead at his home in a suburb of Pittsburgh, in the United States District (Bennsylvania). He would have been on the verge of discovering the source of this epidemic and giving the results of his research. In this confrontation, which has been put to good use by the corona virus crisis, the world order appears without clear sovereignty. World leaders (United States, Russia, China and the European Union) must come together at the same table. They must now tackle regional and international problems in the service of man and not in the service of capital.

5. INTERNATIONAL INFLUENCE NETWORKS IN TUNISIA

The events that occurred during the decade 2010-2020 in the Arab world and in Tunisia were largely constructed, and attempts at explanations of all kinds were not lacking, beyond analyzes of regional and national causes, in particular questioning foreign presences. Digital networks and some media first mentioned, under cover of the United States, a possible Israeli impact. The words attributed to Israeli Defense Minister Ehud Barak below have been circulated as follows : «The Arab Spring is nothing less than the fall of the Arab regimes ». «... We love the instability in Arab countries during these times ... The current Arab situation represents a fertile area for the occupation, and in the interests of its interests ». For its part, the newspaper Yediot Aharonot reported that a senior Israeli official went to Tunisia recently to discuss with local authorities and foreign affairs officials the resumption of diplomatic relations between the two countries as well as Israeli tourism in Tunisia. For its part, the newspaper Al-Fajr claimed that Syrian refugees who entered Algeria were spies for Israel, quickly left for Tunisia after the security blo-cus found in Algeria.

In the same context, Hebrew Radio Rich Pitt revealed that spy Jonathan Pollard, convicted in the United States for spying for Israel, allegedly gave the Israeli Mossad information on Arab countries (their weapons plans, including including Pakistan's nuclear program) and not on US secrets. He also said that the same Pollard would have given Israel information about the headquarters of the Palestine Liberation Organization in Tunisia and intelligence reports regarding Syria.Likewise Ahmed Kahlaoui, president of the Maghreb Observatory to criminalize normalization and support resistance, declared : « Tunisia is under multiple and continuous pressures to push it to normalize its relations with the Zionist entity in the part of the wave of agreements that the occupying entity has made with several Arab regimes, more recently the Kingdom of Morocco »[24].

However, he indicated that « the national committee for the support of the Arab resistance and the fight against

---

[24] Published in the Tunisian newspaper Chourouk, December 21, 2020

normalization with Israel will work for the development of a kind of "road map" against normalization in the areas of education, teaching, culture, tourism and other activities, noting that the future conceptions of the Tunisian state must be oriented towards more openness to the Arab world »[25]. The whole of these sources hypothesize that the Israeli intelligence would practice in the Arab countries and for what interests us in Tunisia, a policy of infiltration and alliance aimed at fragmenting Arab societies from the inside and feeding them internal conflicts, hence the interests evoked by the Dayan Center Israeli[26], for having focused for many years his research on what have been called ethnic and sectarian groups and on the existence of Mo-Saic societies in the Arab Mashreq. As such, the researcher Abdullah Zoghbi mentioned in a study on the role of the Mossad - through the « Israeli Dayan Center » - in the Arab countries and particularly in those which revolted against their regime : « The Arab States are confronted with the stage of internal conflicts and with fragmentation ». He gives the example of Sudan, Iraq, Yemen, Somalia and Lebanon, among others.

During the Troika period, American's encounters with Rached Ghannouchi were not without « friendly advice » for Tunisians regarding the need to improve their relations with Israel and open up channels of communication with

---

[25] Ahmed Kahlaoui, « Call to introduce into the text of the Constitution" the prohibition of normalization with the Zionist entity" », published in TAP on 29 - 01 - 2012. URL: https://www.turess.com/ en / tapfr / 117751.

[26] By studying the content analysis method and following the seminars, workshops and research published by the « Dayan Center for Middle East Research », it is easy to diagnose the role played by this center and the entities which are at the base of it his activity. The Maghreb region is one of the priorities of the center's activity at this stage. In the future, despite the competition that the Dayan Center faces from new Israeli centers, it is still at the forefront in terms of research activity and project formulation in the service of Israeli strategy in the Arab region.

Tel Aviv. Ghannouchi would have reassured Israel on this point, during his participation in the World Forum in Davos in January 2012 in a statement to the Voice of Israel radio station. The statement aroused resentment from Hamas, which does not recognize Israel and reject any normalization with its state, but in return maintains close ties to Ennahdha. The State of Qatar is committed to preparing the ground and led the American and Qatari councils to « announce » the position of Rached Ghannouchi which states that « there is no problem for the party Ennahdha with Israel ».

Ghannouchi is also said to have told the American magazine « Weekly Standard » that the new constitution would not include « any article condemning Israel ».

At a December 2011 conference held by Ghanouchi in Washington at the Center for Near East Policy, known as the intellectual mind of American conservatives and Israeli fanatics, Ghannouchi avoided any hostile signs of the 'Hebrew State. He did not hesitate to appoint Khemaies Jhinaoui, who was director of the Tunis office in Tel Aviv from 1996 to 2000, as assistant to the Minister of Foreign Affairs and to his brother-in-law, Rafik Abdel Salam, in the government of the Troika.

Diplomats and experts in international relations viewed it as tacit, principled endorsement of « normalizing relations with Israel ». This « approval » was confirmed by Rached Ghannouchi personally asserting that the new Tunisian constitution of 2014 does not provide, contrary to what some political parties had proposed, the criminalization of normalization with Israel[27].

---

[27] Rached Ghanouchi wanted normalization and partnership with Israel. In this sense, on February 12, 2020, he sent Howard Cohen, President and CEO of the American-Israel Public Affairs Committee (IBAC), the American-Israeli public affairs commission in Washington, a letter in which he wishes to standardize and connection with the State of Israel. This letter, translated from Arabic, was published by political activist Mondher Guefrach. He confirms on

Without wishing to pass a value judgment on the nature of Tunisia's relations with the State of Israel, we note that they constitute a major issue in international relations. The symbolic structure underlying them stems from the relations of domination established by the Israeli colonization over the Palestinian people, whose headquarters of the Liberation Organization (PLO) has long resided in Tunisia. It was then that an amalgam was formed, both in fact and in opinion, between Zionism and what has been called the Jewish lobby. Confusion was thus created both in Europe and in Tunisia and elsewhere, between Ju-Daism (religion) and Zionism (the State of Israel), and the first (the Jews) was confused with the second (Zionist imperialism). At the same time, the American support for Tunisia was entangled in the mistrust or even the refusal of Tunisian opinion towards the State of Israel, and the amalgamation is now often made between the support of Ghannouchi as well as of a fringe of his Ennahdha party with American interests, and a support, which might seem paradoxical, of this Islamist party for what is called « the American Jewish lobbies ». In this sense, an article from the media site, *hilalpost.com* evoked a « suspicious » relationship between Ghannouchi and the Zionist-American lobby, under the title « Zionist relations of the Tunisian Ennahdha movement ».

The same *hilalpost.com* site indicated that, under the coordination of Radwan Masmoudi, a Tunisian-American working at the CSID (Center for the Study of Islam and

---

that date that the Ennahdha movement stands out from the statements of President Kais Said anti-Israel and underlines that « the presidency of Parliament and the leader of the ruling party will not be authorized to pass a law to criminalize normalization with Israel in Parliament, and that the Ennahdha movement has not given up on its previous commitments ». He said that « the movement's commitment is a clause in the new constitution for normalization with Israel », and that the Ennahdha movement is under no obligation to take up President Kais Said's speech against normalization with Israel.

Democracy), a number of moderate Islamists, Saida Akremi, wife Noureddine Bhiri and Ziyad Daoulatli, as well as Slaheddine Jourchi, known as a « left Islamist », requested an interview with the American ambassador in Tunisia on August 21, 2006. And this in order to ask the United States to support human rights activists, assist in the release of political prisoners, include moderate Islamists on the list authorized to travel to the United States, as well as visit an Islamist residing in the city of Sousse (Hammadi Jebali, who became prime minister in 2012). *Source, WikiLeaks classified document*. Add to this the fact that the two participants of the Troika, Rached Ghannouchi and Moncef Marzouki, first president of the first post-revolutionary republic, received on November 26, 2012 the prize of the influential British organization Chatham house. *Source: confidential document from Welix website*. After the revolution, the leaders of the En¬nahdha party, in particular Rached Ghannouchi, visited several other international and American organizations in particular, « the WINEP - Washington Institute for Near East Policy », and « Saban Center for Middle East Policy ». The sites we have consulted on this point link most of these organizations to large American Jewish families who they believe are linked to Zionist interests.

Finally, when we talk about the networks of international influence on Tunisian political actors, mention is sometimes, but discreetly, made of Freemasonry networks. Freemasonry is a movement considered secret, spread around the world and aimed at controlling it by forging strong links with the leaders of local communities and people of professional or political influence. Its organizations carry out their intellectual and political activities to penetrate the articulations of power through leaders and senior officials helped by the movement to reach high positions in return for serving their goals and keeping their alliances. Its followers describe it as an organization that constitutes a « state within a state ». This has led analysts to view Freemasonry as an extension of what has been called a hidden world government.Popularized in the 18th century, it has been defined as a worldwide fraternal movement whose goals are mutual aid, friendship, kindness and love of people. It is conceived as an « initiatory order which asserts its vision of the world, its humanist philosophy, its social and moral ideal type, its aid for the progressive development of humanity »[28]. While for some it is liberal and secular, for others it aims to spread through the teachings of Satanism and by preparing for the emergence of Antichrist and Judaism.

As far as the Arab world is concerned, Freemasonry would have been established under European colonial influences with certain political elites. Digital networks identify a presence of Freemasonry in Arab countries, 70.000 in Algeria, 250.000 in Egypt, Morocco and Tunisia. But today in the Arab world, it is most often assimilated to Judaism and by derivative to Zionism, the « servants of Satan », and comes under what has been called in the world the « complot theory ». According to this theory, the organization would be supervised by the Rothschilds, and its followers would work for the « Israeli entity ». In the Arab world, Masonry would be criticized for having declared war on religions, and particularly on Islam. Freemasonry would then collect Jewish thought to spread secularism and specifically to fight Islam and the Arabs. On November 28, 1984, the Egyptian Al-Azhar University published a fatwa which reads : « A Muslim cannot be a Masonic because his association with Freemasonry is a gradual departure from the rituals of his

[28] Khalifa Chater, « La Franc-maçonnerie en Tunisie à l'épreuve de la colonisation (1930-1956) », *Cahiers de la Méditerranée*, 72 | 2006, 367-375.

religion, which results in polytheism ». For its part, the League of Arab States published its resolution No. 2309, which reads: « The mason-building movement is a Zionist movement, it contributes to the flow of money to Israel and supports its economy and its efforts to war ».

In Tunisia, the emergence of Freemasonry is linked to the influence of Europe on the south. For example, in the days of Ahmed Pasha Bey, many Masonic groups of French and Italian origin came together to operate in secret. According to certain sources, several Tunisian personalities belonged to these groups, including Habib Bourguiba, Mohamed Mzali, Mohamed Masmoudi. Historian Khalifa Chater sees this headlines « Freemasonry as an enigma, maintained by allusive remarks relating to the membership of some Tunisians in this movement, arousing, moreover, public disapproval »[29]. This disapproval is due to the fact that its secular doctrine aims to strip society of the virtuous values of its religion. Paradoxically, however, it was after the revolution and under the auspices of the Tunisian state that Freemasonry continued its activities : a world conference in February 2011 at the Palais des Congrès in Tunis and led by the party. Islamic Ennahdha, visit to Tunis in June 2011 by a delegation from the Mason-nic Forum in Paris with the intention of concentrating a permanent seat on the Tunisian Masonic Forum. Since then, meetings at the highest level have been organized every month at the headquarters of the Rotary Societies in Tunis, and in its suburbs, with the participation of an American delegation and representatives of the French Embassy.

While the crisis does not mean the end of international interdependence, it may nonetheless translate into a trend towards closure, to the detriment of the weakest that national social and economic programs will increasingly have to preserve. Obviously, after the Coronavirus crisis,

---

[29] Ibid.

Tunisia can no longer be « as before ». The main question in this context is how Tunisia and the political parties in particular have learned a lesson from this crisis. For a good recovery in both the economic and political fields, it is necessary to reform the mechanisms in terms of political governance and economic governance, with the aim of stemming as much as possible speculation or all forms of corruption, promoting job creation and reintegrating social development into political development.

THIRD PART

Corruption in all its dimensions

Corruption offends the country at all levels (administrative, political, economic, and financial), and has led to an estimated budget deficit of $ 1.3 billion and inflation of 7% to 12%. Source Ministry of Finance.

1. FINANCIAL CORRUPTION AT THE SUMMIT OF THE STATE

We will return here to two crucial cases of political corruption. On the one hand, Tunisia found itself in 2020 faced with two « dubious » trade agreements with Turkey and Qatar, prompting the parliament to postpone its vote on these agreements, accompanied by accusations by the president of the parliament, Rached Ghannouchi, abusing his authority to allow the two countries to tighten their grip on the Tunisian economy as part of a political agenda linked to the project of his Ennahdha party. These two agreements with Turkey and with the « Qatar Fund for Development »[30] to open a fund management office in Tunisia, have been described as « colonial » by

[30] « Qatar Fund for Development is a government entity of the State of Qatar, which is responsible for Qatar's international development and foreign aid ». URL: https://en.wikipedia.org/wiki/Qatar_Fund_for_Development

the Tunisian press serving the interests of Qatar and Turkey more than those of Tunisia, and damaging the sovereignty of the country. These agreements indeed allow Turkish institutions to appropriate real estate and land in Tunisia, and violate certain prohibitions on foreigners from owning real estate in Tunisia. It should be specified in this sense, that the President of Parliament, Rached Ghannouchi, exploited the coronavirus crisis and « broke the laws to pass dangerous projects » on the country without obligation to account.

On the other hand, the leader of the Islamist Ennahdha party, Rached Ghannouchi is accused of having used his parliamentary position to make a fortune. Some sources accuse him of holding 40% of most of the loans granted to Tunisia during the revolutionary period. These same sources also specify that the value of his accounts in Swiss banks is strictly confidential, and that most of the Ennahdha party funds are in his name. His fortune is estimated at 4.9 billion dollars. Following the accusations and strong protest from opposition parties in parliament, public opinion rallied for the signing of a petition demanding an audit of President Rached Ghannouchi's fortune. These elements should be placed in the context of the crisis that the Islamist Ennahadha party is currently experiencing. It is in this context that we can read the resignation, on May 26, 2020, of Abdelfattah Mourou, vice-president of the Ennahdha party, a former candidate in the last presidential elections. He felt then that he had not been sufficiently supported by his party. Despite the announcement by Mourou that his resignation has nothing to do with the tensions of the Islamic movement, the truth is that he did not want to « lose face », wanted to preserve himself and show himself outside of all the excesses committed by Ghannouchi, the leader of the movement. In the same context, Abdelfattah Mourou announced his resignation from the Movement a few days after the emergence of a statement by a group within Ennahdha calling itself « The Group of Unity and renewal ». This group was trying to correct the trajectory of the movement, to make a change of direction, so as not to restore confidence in its leader Rached Ghannou-chi, for another term in this post.

Here we can bring together and compare two different logics of family corruption in Tunisia. In comparison, the dynasty of Rached Ghannouchi and his hegemony, as well as the Trabelsi family of Leila Ben Ali, wife of the former head of state, and Zine El Abidine Ben Ali, relies on a logic of corruption. For his part, Ben Ali, despite his authoritarianism and despite his fortune usurped since his seizure of power, was in a process of aid and in « the policy of the outstretched hand » vis-à-vis the population and in particular that of the « gray areas » in the depths of the suburbs and the country. He said he « assisted » the most disadvantaged with an aid program (Fonds de solidarité nationale), justifying the « institutional solidarity »[31] developed for the benefit of this category. This fund, created at the end of 1992, was based on the collection of donations often « imposed » on different groups of citizens to finance economic and social projects, fight against poverty, create jobs in order to improve the financial situation care for the poor and low-income families. Today, for its part, the « Ghannouchi family » is spreading all over the country, not to serve different social categories, but to "indoctrinate" social groups and make them supporters of Enahdha.

The question could be summed up as follows : How can we sanction and fight against the scourge of corruption in a country where the leaders of political parties defend the interests of monopolists (in particular food merchants supported by the administration to escape the sanctions)

---

[31] Houda Laroussi, *Micro-crédit et lien social.* Ibid.

then undertake to define the government strategy ? In this regard, it can be said that corruption has affected social stratification and spread like the Corona virus, everywhere in the cogs of the administration. For example, a government spokes woman on April 25, 2020, revealed crimes of fraud and local interference by political parties in the distribution of in-kind social assistance due to the Corona crisis. Along the same lines, the leader of an opposition party revealed the involvement of accredited agents (local officials) affiliated with the Ennahdha party in providing financial assistance to families known to be loyal to the movement, stressing : « Ennahdha travels regionally to gain trust, whether through social benefits or through food distribution ». Likewise, activists and media have accused a number of Ennahdha leaders of pressuring government officials responsible for determining the destination of social assistance, threatening to dismiss the local head of the Delegation of Fouchana because of his refusal to involve the Islamic movement in distributing government aid.

2. PETTY CORRUPTION AND PARALLEL MARKET

Finance, between the hammer of the crisis and the anvil of the black market and money laundering

The Tunisian authorities have missed the opportunity to alleviate the crisis by fighting against the collapse of the dinar that began in 2011 and accelerated during the Troika era. And this despite the 2014 finance law which, among other things, granted the authorization to practice foreign exchange by opening official offices throughout the territory in order to fight against illegal operations which take place more specifically in cross-border areas. Senior financial sector officials believe that this tax procedure, the first of its kind, would have made it possible to limit the illegal practices of parallel financial markets, due to the discrepancy between the dinar exchange rates on the official markets, in order to support the national currency and foreign exchange reserves. However, the approach of this law has mostly remained unapplied.

To stem this apocalyptic situation of parallel financial markets, the authorities have considered, but without actually taking action, launching a massive campaign against currency traders on the black market in the coming period, in order to create the better conditions for the opening of exchange offices, which must retain the currency monopoly. Likewise, this government has formally undertaken to follow the path of reforming the financial system, by controlling all monthly and annual revenues centralized at the Ministry of Finance, as well as those paid in cash. In theory, these measures are associated with the obligation to have a bank card for anyone whose income exceeds 600 dinars, with a maximum amount of 50 dinars in cash. In addition, for all private and public companies and institutions, salaries should be paid by bank transfer, as should all sales that exceed 1000 dinars. Civil servants, for their part, benefit from the privileges granted by the governments of the Troika after the revolution. At the same time, entire categories of the population have become impoverished in recent years and months. Their purchasing power has diminished considerably. However, in a particularly hypocritical way, the political elite continues to draw the attention of Tunisians to the gravity of an economic crisis for which, despite their stated intentions, they offer no solution.

The « promotion » of the black market

The black market in Tunisia includes commercial transactions in which all tax and trade laws are avoided. This market is directly harmful to the economy, as the transaction rate can reach 60% or more, for example concerning electronic equipment, auto parts or fuels, cigarettes and drugs, imported from Algeria. Monetary transactions are carried out in euros at the border. The size of the black market is smaller in countries with greater economic freedom, and stronger in societies where corruption is most developed. These goods are often smuggled, entered the national market without being registered in official institutions such as the competent customs authority. Corruption has always existed in Tunisia, but increased considerably after the revolution. It could at times have taken other forms under the guise of, for example, compensation for former Islamic political activists.

Then there is another black market that occurs when local production and imports are unable to meet domestic demand that exceeds supply. In this case, exhibitors sell rare products at very high prices, to people who will renegotiate them on the basis of higher profits. These offenses are generally not followed by sufficiently dissuasive sanctions (imprisonment, confiscation of goods, penalties higher than the price of the goods seized). Among the consequences of the black market are the lack of tax revenue for the country and the spread of a type of organized economic chaos, which could have a negative impact on the level of public spending in social and productive areas. The fact remains, in the current state of the Tunisian economy, that the black market can provide financial benefits for pauperized classes, for example due to the exemption from taxes of products purchased.

Today billions of dinars are traded in parallel markets to store large quantities of wine and cigarettes, all taxes not collected by the state. At the same time new taxes justify the high prices of all products such as building materials, electricity, water (an increase of 200%). In 2015 numerous losses were suffered by the Electricity and Gas Company. To this must be added the borrowings of Tunisian public institutions from the European Union in hard currencies, which increased sharply between 2015 and 2019.

In this context, we can say the impotence of public policies and the need not only for a social and solidarity economy but for the Curriculum of the Social and Solidarity Economy (CUR'ESS) which will adapt to this situation harmful socio-economic.

Speculators and monopolies in the cogs of the state

At a time when the whole world is waging a war to curb the spread of the coronavirus, crisis dealers and monopolists have taken advantage of the country's conditions to invest and multiply their wealth. Many unscrupulous traders took advantage of the Tunisian scramble and the exceptional increase in purchasing power during the month of May to skyrocket the prices of certain materials, such as sterilization products, and to store them others, such as flour, semolina and milk. Economic monitoring teams made 34.700 visits and succeeded in inspecting 3.810 economic violations related to prices, monopolies, counterfeiting and notification of subsidies or fines. Surveillance teams seized 7 tonnes of vegetables, 21,800 eggs, 458 tonnes of flour, 1.115 tonnes of semolina, 30.627 liters of vegetable oil, 65 tons of sugar and 41.000 liters of milk. Some state officials were allegedly involved in these packages.

Monopoly manifests itself not only through smuggling and speculation, but also through financial corruption. The monopoly of a market consists in controlling stocks, commodities in order to manipulate their price. It is about getting the largest market share in a particular industry, and then wanting to charge higher prices. The monopolist is the father of controlling a sufficient number of products subject to supply and demand so that he can determine its price, and therefore increase it. This can happen through several mechanisms. A simple strategy is to buy or stock a large amount of the commodities available for cash sale in certain markets. In times of crisis, the monopolist can acquire a large quantity of commodity, and takes advantage of its shortage in the market to resell it at high prices and derive maximum profit from it. In this sense, there are many attempts to mono-polish the markets through huge deals on commodities, milk, oil and semolina. However, when the price begins to move against the monopolist, any attempt by the monopolist to sell is likely to cause that price to drop significantly. We can clearly see here how a context of crisis for some, such as that of the corona virus, can be diverted for the benefit of others. Corruption not only hampers the national economy, but it restricts international trade and economic relations with European countries. In this sense, according to the words of Patrice Bergamini, Ambassador of the European Union in Tunisia, « hotbeds of corruption encourage bad practices, and their proliferation threatens the success of the experiment Tunisian democratic »[32]. In this perspective, Bergamini indicated that « resistance to Aleca was reverting to monopoly positions and pressure from certain family groups who have no interest in seeing young Tunisian operators speak out and break through ».

[32] Interviewed in French newspaper *Le Monde* on July 09, 2019 about the Comprehensive and Deep Free Trade Agreement (Aleca).

He even referred to these groups as « lobbies », « controlling the Tunisian economy preventing any competition from small businesses and young investors ». We will accept these remarks insisting on the fact that the wealth is concentrated in the hands of a few families who refuse to compete. The European ambassador said the economic transition in Tunisia is not yet complete. In this regard, he referred to the role of Aleca in opening up to competition, eliminating the monopoly of these economic groups, corruption and the black market. Some Tunisian commentators may have considered these remarks by Patrice Bergamini as a violation of diplomatic rules. A spokesperson for the Tunisian Forum for Economic and Social Rights, Romdhan Ben Omar, however clarified that the ambassador's statements are not surprising, given that these words have already been uttered by parties and organizations interested in economic affairs, but « what is strange and surprising is the Tunisian position ».

3. ELEMENTS FOR A UNIVERSITY RESEARCH CENTER ON CORRUPTION IN TUNISIA

Reflecting on corruption simultaneously implies clarifying the concept of corruption and the semantic, social and legal « field » it covers beyond received ideas, media representations, and definitions given by international organizations. Beforehan this will require: on the one hand the constitution of a database from the collection of information and statistics relating to corruption ; on the other hand, the development of specific and appropriate studies according to scientific needs ; and finally the implementation of a communication policy and the provision of information, publications, and even the organization of debates and seminars.

3.1. Documentation and capitalization of the existing

This will involve bringing together, in a database, all the documentation available on the issue. It will not only be a source of information, but it will also serve as the first "field" of investigation for research work. First of all, it will be necessary to carry out an inventory of the work already carried out from near or far on the subject of corruption, with research centers, laboratories and teams, university libraries, international organizations and other institutions. Among the inventory of the first works carried out for this database, we can already quote in a non-exhaustive way :

- Reports carried out by international bodies, for example : World Bank report; OECD report, Integrity Diagnosis in the Economic Legal Framework.
- Reports conducted in Tunisia, for example: Tunisian University Forum (UNDP), analysis of perception of corruption in academia and administration; Tunisian Center for Corporate Governance (barometer for measuring and monitoring opinions and representations of corruption with citizens) ; Tunisian Institute for Competitiveness and Quantitative Studies; 2011 Report of the Investigation Commission on Corruption and Malverization; the files available from the INLUC (National Authority for the Fight against Corruption).
- University work carried out in particular by sociologists (CRDI Ottawa, IRMC / Tunis, on justice and representations of the common good)[33].

From this initial documentation, we will be able to : on the one hand induce definitions of corruption in the literature of the social sciences, in the work of international organizations, in legislation, including the Tunisian one; and on the other hand highlighting from this

[33] We refer to the work of Sihem Najar on digital democracy, and of Imed Melliti and Hayet Moussa on *La justice sociale et le bien commun* (in bibliography).

inventory the gaps in terms of research, and the land to be invested subsequently.

3.2. Approaches to be implemented to better « understand » and explain corruption

A typology of cases and forms of corruption

For a researcher, the idea of corruption is difficult to grasp. It can first be classified according to the sectors in which it occurs: administration, justice, police, politics, public procurement, territorial function and municipalities, economy, town planning, public / private sector relations.

Or according to the forms it takes on a daily basis : lobbying, patronage, political protection, smuggling, delinquency, marginality, bribes, paid services, private use of public material, embezzlement, piston, privilege, abuse of power and favoritism etc. Another possible classification (given in the study *petty corruption : the trivialized danger. Exploratory study on petty corruption in Tunisia*, by the Tunisian association of public controllers)[34] is based on the differentiation between « grand corruption » (political especially in the public service, or economic in large companies), and « petty corruption » called ordinary at the level of implementation in the meeting of officials / users.

A comparison of corruption depending on the context

On such a subject, it is advisable to have a point of view of international comparison. Indeed, a light on the different forms of manifestation of corruption according to the country (comparative experiences), will be able to bring out the specificities of Tunisia (clientelism, public / private markets).

---

[34] *La petite corruption : le danger banalisé. Étude exploratoire sur la petite corruption en Tunisie.* Publication du rapport de l'ATCP, Association tunisienne des contrôleurs publics, 2015.

The documentation and studies collected will thus make it possible to « contextualize » corruption according to the economic, social and cultural specificities of each country and its system of standards. It can be seen transversally as a sign of a pathology which disrupts the system of public order by harming the individual. In this sense, we could establish an interaction correspondence between the corruption that is practiced in institutions and the specific « ethical » (moral) of the agents who are at the base of it. The comparative approach can also lead us to jointly analyze forms of regional governance. To each region (governorate), specific corrupt practices could be attributed, linked to the local culture and to the regional socio-economic and cultural context (cross-border region, port region, isolated areas of the interior etc.).

The construction of indicators for measuring corruption

The university centre's documentation and research actions will also focus on: how to measure corruption, on which instruments and measurement indicators to diagnose. Among the existing instruments, to be identified and whose own effectiveness should be measured, we can cite : evaluations and expert judgments; surveys of the experience and perception of corruption among actors ; synthesis of opinions on the governance of institutions or individuals; other indicators such as interviews, the quota method, hypothesis comparisons, then opinion perceptions and accounts of experience.

3.3. Some proposals for studies or research themes to be carried out by the University Center

- The social origins of corruption
- Smuggling, the parallel market and the informal sector

- Corruption in academia, corruption in health institutions (hospitals, etc.)

- Corruption of political elites, corruption in electoral campaigns and elections.

- Monopolies, lobbying, and tax evasion

- Jobs facing corruption (testimonies, fights): accountants, financial and management controllers, administrators of public and private institutions, then lawyers, judges, police, politicians, trade unionists, journalists.

- Civil society actors (associations, trade unions, digital networks, media, etc.), their role to play in the fight against corruption

- Corruption in the face of the common good: the themes of integrity, representations of the just and the unjust, the point of view of complainants and victims.

- Representations of corruption from international organizations and rating agencies.

FOURTH PART

The Social Economy Curriculum and Solidaire CUR'ESS

It must be recognized that the social and solidarity economy is part of a local economy which guarantees the creation of jobs. Its objective is not for profit, but rather to carry out a collective project, most often with a social purpose. It is an opportunity to build a new approach to development based on the participatory economy and democratic management. This approach requires a diagnosis which is established by the citizen to identify and visualize his own needs, to facilitate the management of his projects. This helps to crystallize, or even strengthen regional spaces with a local identity, and to enhance human and material resources, in order to create activities and create opportunities for working and providing better services to citizens.

The social economy and the services that fall under the solidarity economy are guided and governed by the principles of justice, cooperation, transparency and solidarity. The Fair Trade and Solidarity Trade System, officially approved by the Brazilian President in 2009, is the first staterecognized and supported marketing system in the world.

This sector is currently more likely to succeed in Tunisia due to the development of mentalities, the entrepreneurial culture, the large number of higher education graduates, and the ability to participate voluntarily in all activities provided by components of civil society and non-governmental institutions, in particular associations of various types, cooperatives working in the agricultural field, and the private sector, especially in disadvantaged areas.

What does Tunisia need for the SSE project to succeed ? Legislative initiatives for solidarity and the social economy. The latter are decisive in the success of experiences, many of which have been supported by public institutions, which provide free services to support and assist the sector financially, this was the case for example in the Moroccan experience. Some countries are also promoting the cooperative sector through financial support, based on the financial incentive mechanism, and developing solidarity financing through banks and solidarity funds, to generate social and solidarity projects. In addition, these support organizations (e.g. in Brazil) have contributed significantly to the conversion of the informal sector and parallel trade into an organized sector, at a time when Brazil, with its successful experience, has created a national product marketing agency.

Today, we underline the need to convince politicians and those in charge of the public sectors, that this economic model (SSE, social and solidarity economy) does not present itself as an alternative to the State, nor does it contradicts, but rather that it tries, through its organizations, which are components of civil society, to form links of integration and partnership with the State, especially if it is the State of law and the law.

Before discussing our project below, which concerns a new conception of the social and solidarity economy called the « Curriculum of the social and solidarity economy », CUR'ESS, it is important to return to the roots of the social economy and then to evoke the Tunisian experience in this sector, and in particular to mutualism at the time of Bourguiba, in order to draw lessons from its failure.

In the second section of this part we will suggest the Algerian experience (Algeria chose the same cooperative system after its independence) to better understand the logic of this system and its challenges in a country with we share more or less the socio-economic context. In the other sections, we will make concrete proposals.

1. THE ROOTS OF THE SOCIAL ECONOMY, AND THE REVERSE OF COOPERATIVISM

The roots of the social economy go back to the labor movement of the 19th century and its resistance to the logic of the industrial revolution. Faced with their precarious living conditions, the workers, inspired by utopian socialist thinkers (Saint Simon, Charles Fourier, etc.), organized themselves and set up mutual aid societies, for cooperation between the rich and the poor, food outlets and production cooperatives were created.

As the concept of *social economy* belongs to French researchers who rediscovered it since 1977, and used it to refer to a group of organizations made up of associations and cooperatives, the model has evolved into associate with the concept of solidarity. We mention here the contributions of researchers such as Bernard Eme and Jean-Louis Laville, who are recognized for having defined this alternative economy as a set of activities that contribute to the democratization of the economy, starting with by citizenship obligations [35] . And far from

[35] Bernard Eme, Jean-Louis Laville, *Cohésion sociale et emploi*, Paris, Desclée de Brouwer, 1994.

compensating for the work of the state, it is a collaborative action with public authorities to reintegrate third sector structures into the economy. It is also a social and cultural inclusion project. Consequently, this economic model has assumed great importance, reflected by the large number of research and studies devoted to it in the countries of the North as in the countries of the South.

The social economy contains laws and structures that uphold human priority[36]. The concept has started to gain institutional and legal recognition in many countries of the world to refer to the third sector, and it is necessary to question the current idea that the social and solidarity economy is specific to poor countries. Several countries in the North and the South are adopting this economic model. We take the example of France, Italy, Germany and Brazil, which have developed a law on the social and solidarity economy. In France, the law on the social and solidarity economy was adopted at the end of July 2014. This French law codifies the working rules of specialists in the social and solidarity economy, it gives rigor and legislative recognition to its institutions, structures and tools. SSE plays an important role internationally, both economically and humanly. In Europe and the Arab world, this economy employs more than 14.5 million people. In some countries, such as Belgium, France, the Netherlands and Morocco, the social and solidarity economy contributes more than 10% of the GDP. It allows nearly 15% of the Brazilian population, or about 29 million people, to escape the threshold of poverty. It can be

« The solidarity economy can be defined as the set of production, exchange and distribution activities contributing to the democratization of the economy from civic commitments ».

[36] The social economy contains laws and its constituent structures (associations and institutions), but contrary to what one suggests, capital is a defining component of the social economy. Despite everything these organizations evoke in relation to the purpose of their activities, they defend both human priority and capital as well.

considered as a lever for progress in development, especially after the economic and financial crisis that the world has known since 2008 and which encouraged the United Nations General Assembly to declare 2012 the International Year of Cooperatives, under the slogan « cooperative projects to build a better world ».

In this sense, we will ask the question of what the Tunisian State has been able to bring through its economic and social development policies to job seekers : what are the employment opportunities developed in the public sector and the emerging sector of the social and solidarity economy ? A host of national and international organizations (Enda, Taysir, Yunus social business, Lab'ESS, Prom'ESS, etc.) encourage social entrepreneurship, as a solution for integration into the labor market. What response can this sector provide to young graduates seeking employment ? For the State, the social economy still remains a slogan, used in official speeches, a speech on paper, which unfortunately does not achieve its goal which would be to revitalize the values advocated by the social economy, that is an economy serving the weakest and the most disadvantaged.

The Tunisian experience in solidarity economy in its mutual form in the 1960s failed not for reasons intrinsic to this economy, but because of the adoption of an approach that was poorly managed at the decision-making level and in which the participation, accountability and democracy were absent. Today, we must look at this experience to better understand the causes of his « abortion » and take advantage of it to focus on a unified social economy that promotes sustainable development in its various dimensions and helps to create dynamism within social groups. We evoke the experience of cooperativism after the independence of Tunisia under the regime of the first president Habib Bourguiba, the way in which this initiative was carried, and how this project was conceived at the time, by its Minister of the Economy Ahmed Ben Salah. It is important before going into the details of this experience, to clarify Bourguiba's strategy with regard to this political choice with his minister. Recall that Ah-med Ben Salah, was born in 1926 in Moknine, studied at Sadiki college (melting pot of Tunisian nationalism), then in France. Ben Salah was intellectually built in Europe as part of his trade union experience before his final return to Tunisia, which in fact led him to hold several political responsibilities within Bourguiba's government.

What raises questions here, and what is equivocal, is Bourguiba's attitude and his hostile stance towards Ah-med Ben Saleh and his socialist inclinations, however contradicted by granting him the highest economic responsibility for the country. Bourguiba said in his speech in Egypt in February 1965, trying to explain the stage Tunisia had chosen at the time: « As for private property, we do not see its nationalization in any way. The state continues to run this sector until the workers can manage the means of production themselves and the danger subsides ». He adds, and therefore « the experience of cooperatives conforms to socialist scientific theory with regard to the strengthening of the state in order to be able to control the economy in its various industrial, agricultural and service aspects, with the economic freedom of the people and of the small peasants and of those who have small farms, but this does not exactly mean the congruence with which Marxism was created. Take the term solidarity to avoid the term socialism, because the latter has a negative impact in certain capitalist regimes such as the United States and then France ». It is obvious that the term solidarity (in the associative, even cooperative sense) is closer to Tunisian mentality, and the direct theoretical reference on which Tunisian reciprocity will be based in the sixties.

Led by Ben Salah, the cooperative experiment addressed the need to focus on settlers who seize state resources and assets such as olive trees, steel wheat and phosphate. This was seen as a major step towards the completion of the path of definitive independence and the adoption of cooperative groups to develop means of production which will be supervised by the State in order to guarantee the proper distribution and workers' rights. On the demand side, the tax increase in funding the mutual support policy occurred at a rate of 22.5% in 1962, and it depended mainly on foreign loans, particularly from the United States (from the World Banc) and France, who took advantage of Tunisia's resources for the reconstruction and development of their own countries. This money represented 40% of the total investment in the 1960s, and during this decade the state succeeded in nationalizing almost all the land that became available in August 1969. It is important to stress that the equivalent of 1.762 agricultural cooperatives were built on the basis of 4.110.000 hec-tares which belonged to individuals. These formalities were governed by the administration and through the regional directorates, which were most able to promote the collective and societal interest. These cooperatives have independent activities subject to autonomous, democratic and participatory management, in which the association is free. They proposed models based on an integrated and sustainable economy, producing goods and services centered on the human being as a source of development, and rooted in collective interest groups.

Until now, the failure of the experiment of cooperativism, which can also be called « the experiment of synergy », remains a mystery. Conducted since 1962 by Ahmed Ben Sala h, this experiment had a convincing success in its beginnings and then a failure in 1969, following economic, social and political interactions. This new economy broke with the old practices of Tunisians, but was included in economic strategies aimed at creating a balance between all groups in society and more particularly between the poor and the rich after independence. Why this failure ? In fact, it is an economic system that includes a set of cooperative processes of access to production, escaping individual ownership and coming under the public sector or « collective ownership » and participatory under the auspices of of State. Society thus frees itself from individual property and private economic initiatives. So we understand from the above, that solidarity means the collective ownership of members of society under the auspices of the state which then becomes the one and only engine, manager and controller of the economy. During this period, all sectors and individual and private goods were confiscated and became state property. As a first step, the state creates agricultural production units and cooperative units with the aim of limiting the phenomenon of rural displacement. Then he established industrial poles in all regions of the country, such as the steel industry in Manzel Bourguiba and the tobacco factory in Kairouan. But the Tunisians did not accept this new economic experience, especially the rich. Among trade unionists, it was understood at the time that Ahmed Tlili[37] was the first to point out the error in the mutual support approach in Ahmed Ben Salah's policy, and was against the approach taken. The reason why Tunisians rejected this process, explained by the fact that solidarity constitutes a threat to individual property. The question then is whether solidarity is « driven » by the state to make it its dominant economy, or whether the state makes solidarity the only dominant economy. Here, the

[37] He was one of the political leaders close to Bourguiba. He was part of Neo Destour. By being a trade union leader, he campaigned for respect for human rights. Subsequently, he opposed the Bourguiba regime and distinguished himself by his fierce positions against the ruling powers.

private sector and all forms of individual property are permanently eliminated.

There are also reports confirming that farmers in the central and southern regions of the country have migrated to the mountains and deserts, accompanied by their sheep and camels, for fear that the state confiscates their agricultural properties. Other Tunisians categorically refused to experience solidarity, in particular the large owners of agricultural land, this approach was not considered fair for them and in their opinion unjust : because the non-owners there enjoy the same rights as young and former owners. However, some economists reject this explanation and focus their analyzes on the side of state authoritarianism. The state's strategy was to control, if not dominate, all economic activities, find the means to appropriate all sectors of production and have a monopoly on them through the exploitation of labor. Ahmed Ben Salah's experiment ended in 1969 with failure. After this failure, the country followed liberal economic experiments which, during the 1980s and 1990s, contributed to the recovery of the Tunisian economy. The liberal economy is more efficient because it oscillates between the private and the public sectors. The failure of the experiment of « sympathy » of cooperativism led the former Tunisian minister Ahmed ben Salah to be exempted from his functions and imprisoned by order of President Habib Bourguiba until his escape from prison in 1973.

In fact, solidarity is seen as an unsuccessful economic model during this period because it denies individual property and private initiatives.

On the pooling policy of former Minister Ahmed Ben Salah

In his testimonies [38], Ahmed Ben Salah evokes the foundations of his political experience of mutualisation at the time of Bourguiba, and the « revolution » he wanted to lead in the agricultural sector. He explains that following negotiations established with France in the early 1960s, 150,000 hectares of agricultural land were recovered mainly in northwestern Tunisia. The dominant crop in these regions is based exclusively on large grains (wheat, barley, flour). Most of this land was under colonial rule or bought at the lowest prices. This means that a large part of the farmers with small and medium plots have been stripped of their properties. It is important to point out that the north is exceptional in the production of wheat in particular and therefore supposed to be one of the most prosperous regions of the country. As has never been the case, this means that these regions were not benefiting from their agricultural production.

Ben Salah's goal was to revive agriculture after the country's independence, and to diversify its production. Moreover, this reform and diversification cannot be done in dispersed areas. The most salient problem of the time, according to Ben Salah, was the « scattering of property », even of plots. This dispersion neglected the diversity of agriculture, and the first attempt to remedy it after the recovery of thousands of hectares was the creation of « synergies », that is to say groups of small farmers gathered around a large plot of the reclaimed land, so that the mutualism consisted of a relatively large land. And we are at the heart of mutualism since it is a question of « pooling agricultural resources » in order to « share risks » and put them « in the charge of a community, a collectivity, resources

[38] *Témoignage d'Ahmed Ben Salah sur son parcours national et international*, Fondation Temimi pour la recherche scientifique et l'information, Zaghouan, 2002

within a solidarity network »[39]. In this case, the notions of sharing and cooperation are the basis of Ben Salah's project.

This attempt to regroup, at the time, stems from the difficulty of the owners of small plots who cannot produce crops and vegetables because this requires loans, which the bank cannot grant to « small » farmers. On this basis, 15 mutual support groups were formed in the governorate of Kef, in the north-west, but without this being adapted to administrative or legal procedures. In other words, this regrouping project was conceived outside any legal text. This is a choice made so that the problem of deterrence or pressure does not arise. This was a way to help small owners to join the mutual, without losing possession of their land, suddenly each farmer preserved his land. Finally, the mutual has become a business between farmers who keep their individual property deeds and benefit from the area with which each contributes to the mutual. Thus, a democratic model is imposed through mutual support, based on the fact that each has a role, and each has a voice in the conduct and choice of cultures. This was the mutual model that Ahmed Ben Salah championed for the benefit of smallholder farmers. This model was decided in collaboration with all these farmers who adapted it. Remember that the large landowners did not agree with this choice and refused to participate in the project with the small « peasants ». In his testimonies, Ben Salah explains that the law would be a means to oppress all those who refused to associate and that would lead to repression. In addition, funds were collected in order to grant them within the framework of cooperative loans to small farmers who are part of the mutuals. However, even those who refused to join the mutuelles (for a geographical reason) benefited from these loans. Ahmed Ben Salah had formed some forty funds, which he considered to be an achievement at the time, because he wanted to show very simply that mutuals were an opportunity to review working conditions in the agricultural sector and in all regions of the country.

[39] Cyrille Devendeville, « Les aspects généraux de la mutualisation », *Gazette des archives*, pp. 33-40, 2013.

Subsequently, « pilot » experiments began to bear fruit almost everywhere. In this sense, the planting of tomato plots in Kef has been a successful experience. At the same time, another successful project, still in the region, consisted of cultivating fish in the Mallègue[40] valley, for the benefit of the inhabitants of the region 300 production units were grouped together in the northwest and six million olive trees were planted, and it was following these experiences that the World Bank granted funding.

Ben Salah highlighted the difficulties encountered at the beginning in obtaining funds from the World Bank, which is reluctant to projects in the agricultural sector, which refused to grant a loan for this Tunisian project. He therefore proposed that he set up a tripartite committee (World Bank, Food and Agriculture Organization of the United Nations (FAO), and senior official of the Tunisian government) to study his request and finance universities. Mutual productive tees in the north-west of Tunisia. The committee was set up in Tunisia, its members visited the production units and discussed with the farmers. A loan of $ 18 million followed in 1964 to finance the 300 units. This is the WB's first funding experience for this type of project, both in Tunisia and in the world. The success of these projects marked the start of the agricultural industry in Tunisia. In the foreign press, particularly in Tunisia, we speak of « collectivism » when, for Ben Salah, it is « economic and cooperative work ».

It must be recognized that the experience of solidarity began with the establishment of productive units in the governorate of Kef. It was after this successful experience that efforts were made throughout the republic. Ben Salah wanted to encourage the diversification of agriculture on the basis of state contribution. Its strategy was based on a basis of equality between what the state can do and what the private sector demands or can provide. According to him, the

---

[40] The valley of Mallègue is « 130 kilometers flowing in the west of Tunisia. Its watershed is partly in Algeria ».
URL: https://fr.wikipedia.org/wiki/Oued_Mell%C3%A8gue

approach of the agricultural project was based on the freedom of membership. In his testimony, Ben Salah made it clear that mutual support is not the property of the state, and that the agricultural mutual is not a constraint for farmers. In other words, it was not an act forced by the state.

Why did this mutual project go wrong then ? It was, according to Ben Salah, a successful peasant revolution. However, the failure would have been borne by political advisers close to Bourguiba who pushed the president to generalize productive regrouping throughout the country. For President Bourguiba, mutualism was an opportunity to improve the living conditions of poor peasants, and also a methodology for « supervising » the populations. Ben Salah was against this authoritarian political project of generalization. Rather, Ben Salah's wish was to reform peasant working conditions and adapt these reforms to various regions. Subsequently, Bourguiba expressed his change of position when he called for the agricultural cooperation law to be presented to the assembly.

2. THE SOCIAL ECONOMY, A RESPONSE TO THE CRISIS AFTER THE INDEPENDENCE OF ALGERIA

Tunisia is not the only one to have followed this mode of economy. Algeria, for its part, has lived the experience. Former Algerian President Houari Boumediene established a program based on the value of solidarity after his country gained independence. For Boumediene, solidarity was one of the most enduring civilizational values that have their roots in the history of the company. These roots extend to Berber tribal origins in Algeria in terms of belonging and spontaneous social contract, to deepen further with the spread of Islam. This restored to the habits of solidarity their spiritual depth, while their contractual dimension has continued through legislation and jurisprudence. As part of the legal and fiscal measures taken by Algerian society after its independence, in addition to the nationalization of settler lands and the appropriation of European companies, « the Algerian government sought what was in Algiers bourgeoisie ; it also appealed to individuals by creating a national solidarity fund supplied by donations »[41]. This is how the work on the value of solidarity began in Algeria. What was the approach adopted by Boumediene for the implementation of this project ? What are the consequences for the national economy ?

To understand the approach adopted by the Algerian government which has chosen to develop a cooperative and united project, it is necessary to grasp the historical context which fostered the emergence of this experience. Unquestionably, the situation in Algeria stabilized after the turmoil that followed a military coup led by Colonel Houari Boumediene, Minister of Defense, against President Ahmed Ben Bella on June 19, 1965. All pockets of the remaining resistance of the « local forces », which are militias formed by the overthrown president, were confronted with the army as needed. And its presence as a parallel army was one of the main weapons of the coup. The leading group led by Colonel Boumediene, commander-in-chief of the army during the War of Independence, resisted but its men were scattered.

The colonel gathered his comrades in the « Council of the Revolution », and declared to them : « The situation is serious, the people we control them but we do not rule, because the one who governs must have a program and must be aware of how to build the country he governs ». A long discussion took place, and everyone opened the way : first, we must calm the spirits by adopting a discourse of unity, not of rebellion, and by continuity, not

[41] Roger Le Tourneau, « Le Maghreb d'antan a-t-il connu des révolutions ? », *Revue des mondes musulmans et de la Méditerranée*, 1968, pp. 153-160.

estrangement, and by union, not division. The president of the « Revolutionary Council » contacted diplomat and lawyer Mohamed Seddik Benya-hia, who had been appointed Algerian ambassador to Moscow some time ago. An urgent meeting took place between the two men, during which Benyahia supports the decision of the revolutionary leadership to form a working group « in order to present a program for the renaissance of the Algerian state in various sectors ». Boumediene had great faith in the man who had helped found the « General Union of Algerian Muslim Students » in July 1955, and was among the most important organizers of the student uprising and high schools for join the armed struggle. One of the first works of this working group was the « Triple Plan 1967/1969 » which was built on three pillars : the expansion of scientific and technological education, building an industrial base and agricultural reform.

Depending on the priorities, the work team grew larger over the days. It began to cover all specialties and evolved into a « socio-economic council », drawing up development plans and playing the role of Parliament in the submission of bills. Thanks to this policy, Algeria emerged from its difficult situation to acquire an important industrial base and control its wealth after the nationalization of all French property, its rehabilitation and its modernization. The ambition of the Algerian government was the establishment of a new agricultural system called « The agricultural revolution », with the slogan « The land for those who serve it », in response to the country's need to overcome a stifling crisis in the city and an unprecedented urgency of agricultural work in the countryside. Hundreds of thousands of families have left the countryside to settle in towns where there is school, hygiene, work and lighting. The countryside had become a vast arena of poverty and underdevelopment for almost 500 years, from the Ottoman rule which pressed people with taxes, to the French rule which seized the most beautiful lands and took them away distributed to European settlers. And that until a fierce war that rural people endured for more than seven years, during which they suffered murder and displacement.

During the first years of independence, towns were populated by rural residents until they could no longer receive them, schools were no longer sufficient and water, electricity and sanitation networks did not fulfill their function. Belts of misery were formed by tin houses on the outskirts of towns, and others built on the roofs of buildings left by the occupation. In the late sixties, a team of experts devoted search for an answer to an urgent question : « Why do the villagers abandon their land and come back to the city ? » and they found the answer thus : « They come for the well-being, because the situation in the countryside is overwhelming ». Well-being then had to be transferred to the countryside for people to settle there. The government immediately began to work on completing the larger project, and so the « agricultural revolution » was born. This is followed by the construction of a thousand peasant towns with all their facilities. The houses are distributed to the farmers and the land is allocated to them free of charge in the form of collective cooperatives, starting with those of the state inherited from the nationalized occupation farms, as well as the unused land. In the 1970s, the Algerian was angry when his country was compared to Spain or South Korea. Its horizon was wider there, as the middle class grew there, offering great opportunities to form a strong elite.

However, many believe that the « agricultural revolution » project has historically been much higher than the level reached by Algerian society. The cooperative system is complicated to manage and requires other levels of awareness, coexistence and the ability to work together. Unfortunately, a large number of officials who had great responsibilities did not understand the project to the point that it evaporated immediately after the death of President Houari Boumediene.

3. FOR ANOTHER ECONOMY: THE SOCIAL AND SOLIDARITY ECONOMY CURRICULUM (CUR'ESS)

Tunisia has experienced development through liberal mode at the start of independence, cooperativism in the 1960s and then a return to liberalism in the 1970s and to this day. However, the country today finds itself facing economic and financial difficulties not only linked to the current international situation and the fallout from the Coronavirus, but also to the complex social situation in which a category is plunged. Population. In this sense, it is important to remember that the country has one million and seven hundred thousand poor (1.700.000), as well as an unemployment rate that reaches 17.5%. There are 500.000 Tunisians, who live on 4 dinars a day, and in particular vulnerable families below the poverty line who represent 17% of the total population, or around one million Tunisians. This category is much more noticeable and even specific in some regions that suffer from exclusion and marginalization, more than others. The most marked regions are located in the North-West and Center-West, such as the governorate of Kairouan [42], whose unemployment rate exceeds 35%, the governorates of Siliana, and Kef which also have high unemployment.

[42] Kairouan is a city in central Tunisia. It is located 150 kilometers southwest of Tunis, the capital.

Unemployment rate in Tunisia

The unemployment rate in Tunisia during the current year (2020) is 15.3%, registering a slight decrease of 0.1 point (15.4% compared to 2018 and 0.2 point compared to the previous year), with the same drop in unemployment for holders of higher diplomas during this year. The number of unemployed registered for the year 2019, according to the National Institute of Statistics, is 637.7 thousand unemployed, against 644.9 thousand in 2018. The unemployment rate this year for men is estimated at 12.4% (stable compared to the same period in 2018) and at 22.6% for women, down 0.1% compared to the previous year. As for the unemployment of higher education graduates, the number of those unemployed in this category fell to 255.4 thousand at the end of March this year from 261.1 thousand last year. Since 2018, it has fallen by around 5.7 thousand unemployed, a decrease of 28.2%, compared to 29.3% in the same period of 2018.

The unemployment rate in some Tunisian governorates is distributed as follows. The governorate of Tataouine 32%, Gafsa 25%, Ke¬bili 25.9%, Tozeur 20.9%, Jendouba 20.1%, The governorate of Tunis 19.5%, Beja 18.5%, Siliana 17.2%, Kairouan 15.8%, Sidi Bouzid 15.4%, Sousse 12.6%, Ariana 11.6%, Mahdia 12,%, Le Kef 11.1%, Na¬beul 10.3%, Médenine 9.9%, Sfax 9.8%, Monastir 6.6%.

Consequently, many voices defend the idea of a social and solidarity economy which can provide solutions within the framework of a new vision of development in all fields and for all types of activities, based on freedom, dignity, justice and solidarity. Many therefore plead for a solidarity economy modeled on the models of other countries. However, the current situation requires a model that is also inspired by successful experiences in the world, but that is unique to adapt to the Tunisian reality in its logic and in its entanglements. This new economy would make it possible both to respond to the crisis of employment and mass unemployment as well as to poverty, but also to fight against the growing phenomenon of the black economy, smuggling, monopoly and money laundering. Its central principle is to emphasize « the priority of man and the value of labor at the expense of profits and not of capital ». As well as « common interest over individual interest », « non-discrimination », « freedom of engagement », and « independence » are criteria that must be shared. The basic rule of this new approach concerns democratic management: by adopting the principle of a vote equal to one person. In this sense, it aims mainly, in addition to the promotion of employment, to achieve a balance between the requirements of economic viability and the values of social solidarity, the dedication of social justice, the equitable distribution of wealth, achieving integrated growth for the benefit of all groups.

From this perspective, the Tunisian experience must take into account two principles: take advantage of past and lay a solid foundation for the future. Some experts suggest that we currently have to rely on our own resources and on ourselves. This requires changing the concept of the social economy, on a solid basis to « save what remains to be saved ». This is why the country must assume its responsibilities and act under the supervision of educational advisers and skills in human and social sciences, capable of participating in the development of the sector, in the sharing of responsibilities and consultation especially with the youngest entering the market.

Our ***Curriculum de l'Economie sociale et solidaire (CUR'ESS) project***, which we detail below (sub-parts 4 and 5), consists of a provisional listing in order to propose a first development of objectives, strategies and support institutions according to a participatory economic approach. Institutions that meet the following two conditions in terms of social protection.

First: Stronger global security. The new conception of CUR'ESS will include groups of distinguished people who will work within an institution. The latter must have extensive experience, in order to cover all the risks incurred by the populations, in a manner complementary to the legal systems of social security and health coverage, then in order to provide assistance services within the framework of solidarity and cooperation, for the benefit of the people involved and their first right in exchange for salaries and contributions.

Second : The right to insurance. Cooperative insurance companies are civil societies that must fulfill their obligations to cover the risks incurred by policyholders, depending on the nature and status of the projects concerned. In other words, the CUR'ESS aims to ensure health coverage for all workers who are no longer in the labor market. Everything here toyen has the right to health insurance. Every Tunisian has the right to medicine, education, and a respectable monthly income. In this sense, social coverage, while working to improve the condition of vulnerable groups, will extend to all professional groups. The social security system must take into account the financing capacities, in other words the contributions of all groups in society (and not only the State employees who are already beneficiaries), and guarantee them a minimum of benefits social (health coverage, old age, work accidents and occupational diseases). Today, many homeworkers or farmers do not receive the health coverage indicated in the texts. These groups are exploited by private companies and landowners who, despite their capital and resources, refuse to pay the payroll taxes of their employees.

It should be specified in this sense that the CUR'ESS must not be part of traditional practices, nor of a welfare state. On the one hand, traditional societies and tribal groups have known what is called social solidarity, in the forms of cooperative life, solidarity and equality between individuals during the different agricultural seasons. The local community, for example, organized the harvest of dates, olives, or other work requiring cooperation between different individuals and even between the owner and the employees. All this confirms a basic community solidarity. On the other hand, if the Tunisian state must be able to carry out « a cooperative economic policy », this can no longer refer strictly to the previous experiences of the 1960s, described above. Several historical, economic and sociological readings of the 1960s describe them as arbitrary and authoritarian in the political and economic history of Tunisia.

It is essential to approach a new « mode of economic, social and united development », through the results of research, scientific seminars and according to the conditions of economic development in which the State has conducted its policy in certain cases periods. It is now a question of making a « new economic, scientific and intellectual proposal » with the participation of associations, and certain national organizations, not to mention the Tunisian General Labor Union. With the support of all these actors, the social and solidarity economy could be considered in addition to the public and private sectors, as a third sector of the Tunisian economy, particularly active in terms of reducing unemployment and poverty. In this sense, the will of the state will be decisive. On June 17, 2020, the Tunisian parliament adopted the draft law on the social and solidarity economy in order to balance economic growth and social equity on the basis of a legal framework proposed by the UGTT, and support from the ILO.

Thus, the two basic pillars of the project that we are proposing would be: a legal text validated by the

Assembly of People's Representatives (ARP), and support institutions (cooperatives, private companies, etc.). These two pillars would impose themselves as safeguards or beacons in order to favor legal access to employment and simultaneously reduce the unemployment of graduates or the recourse to informal activities or even smuggling. In this case in an international context where the constitutions of many countries have extended the SSE to the most deprived categories of society, we believe that the proposals of our CUR'ESS project, presented in the pages following, aim to establish the SSE by extending it to sectors not covered to date, and more precisely relating to what is today imposed on the margins as a fourth sector, that of the informal economy or even of smuggling and petty corruption. This so called informal sector could then more easily fit into the third sector proposed by a new conception of SSE coming to coexist with the so-called public and so-called private sectors. We will see that CUR'ESS will advocate strict laws in order to limit the phenomena of tax evasion and cross-border smuggling, mentioned previously, like what is practiced at the Algerian border. In this sense, a social and united economy would make it possible to absorb the so-called informal sector, and would become the third pillar on which a balanced and integrated economy would be built, with the public sector and the private sector. This third economy has the capacity and the means to mobilize itself to provide better social cohesion, open to the participation of all social classes and businesses from different sectors.

4. OBJECTIVES AND CONDITIONS OF THE COURSE

To do this, the state will have to play a new role. And this of course with the contribution of the Ministry of Vocational Training and Employment, able to organize seminars and support the government position on this new economic approach. In this sense, as a host State, it will have the task of promoting the training courses that will be organized in the field of CUR'ESS, of re-examining employment and sector policies, on the basis of documented studies and of listening sessions with the various stakeholders, such as the unemployed entering or graduating from higher education, civil society associations, and social workers. Through this economic project, the success of CUR'ESS will be supported by experiences and pilot models, both national and international, not necessarily transferable but likely to provide points of support for the construction of this third sector. However the condition for this new role to play of a host State, remains its homogeneous adherence, followed by that of its administration, to the desire to recompose the current informal sector occupied by monopolists, smugglers, traffickers, money launderers, and all those who exploit the country's resources.

1. The objective of CUR'ESS in its current form is to stimulate economic, social and solidarity institutions for all job seekers. It must materialize through its integration into the draft law of June 17, 2020 on SSE. In this sense, it is essential to revise, and make suggestions if necessary, to the bill, and this under the aegis of a group of experienced specialists, and the following proposals.

2. It is necessary that the role of the State be clearly defined in CUR'ESS, and that it be part of a long-term vision and strategy on CUR'ESS, which allow the advancement of the project with a new solidarity economy.

3. This vision and strategy of the State will have to be conceived in a participatory framework which includes all the parties concerned, in particular the active civil society in the field, to guarantee the consent of all the partners on its content, otherwise the CUR'ESS will become a text without effectiveness or feasibility.

4. The program activates the new solidarity economy in many sectors, such as agriculture, traditional industries, transport, health and services, which depend on sector ministries. As such, the creation of an intersectoral ministry in charge of ESS and CUR'ESS would be an advantage in establishing ministerial overlap in the conduct of this new approach.

5. During negotiations on employment in the country, it would be necessary to keep the register of unemployment numbers in localities, delegations and regions.

6. State funding for the benefit of small farmers will be made subject to reports at the end of the year to accompanying trainers and experts providing professional follow-up. The financing of the large peasantry will be provided by the landowners or with the participation of companies (agro-food, tec exports, etc.). The wages of workers in both sectors will be indexed to end-of-year profits and not to capital.

7. Companies under the ESS must be removed from the trade register because it meets the requirements of private or sectoral institutions with a special accounting system, while the ESS is part of another approach solidarity market economy. Institutions specific to this 3rd sector must not be juxtaposed with those of the other two (public and private).

8. Considering that most of the companies active in the field are small, it is proposed to guarantee their success, the increase of the percentage of profit distribution within the limit of a quota of 50%.

9. The law in its current form and content is irrelevant to the sector as it will interfere with the legal texts that govern mutuals, societies, cooperatives and the new approach. It is therefore more useful in this case to update the legal texts of these institutions and to include a chapter on the principles of CUR'ESS after having been approved by the government and the ARP.

10. The associations are not part of the institutions of the new solidarity economy program, of the new solidarity economy program, according to the bill of June 17, 2020. This should be remedied because this could exclude the institutions currently active in the field.

11. CUR'ESS is part of the objective of: job creation, the establishment of partnerships between the poor and the rich, and social cohesion in order to contribute to economic growth. Its strategies are the integration of different social groups, and the shift from the informal economy, the fourth sector, to the third sector, that of SSE. The state will have to integrate all of these objectives precisely.

12. Advocate the granting of a loan for the creation of micro-enterprises with an interest rate that does not exceed 7% by integrating the follow-up services offered. This funding will be supervised by the first person in charge (CEO) within the new ministry in charge of the economy and solidarity.

13. Establishment of a higher council « Supreme Council for the New Social and Solidarity Approach » which includes all partners, in particular representatives of civil society, funding institutions, and academics. The composition of this board, its tasks and its operating methods are determined by government decrees under the supervision of the CEO within the new ministry in charge of the economy and solidarity or the new approach solidarity and social.

5. STRATEGIES FOR THE REBUILDING OF THE ECONOMY IN THE FRAMEWORK OF THE CUR'ESS

The new model of the social and solidarity economy advocated here will be based on scientific bases capable of providing civil society with a strong fluency in all areas,

« so that we can progress towards the goal step by step, using ingenuity and effort to do so »[43], Habib Bourguiba said. In order to fight against informal profits, this social and economic recovery will take place under the following strategic conditions.

1. The establishment of self-sufficient development, which should suspend all imports related to unnecessary products, for a period of 3 years to 5 years. In this perspective, it would be advisable to review certain clauses of contracts concluded with European countries for 30 years.

2. The economy would be aligned with the production of national products, especially agricultural products. In this case, all land must be cultivated (wheat, barley, vegetables and fruits, depending on the specificity of the regions).

3. Any citizen who monopolizes local products to transport them to cross-border countries (Libya, Algeria) or to increase prices, will be brought to justice.

4. To deal with the financial accumulation resulting from underground, a presidential decree will have to be issued for the central bank to print new money.

5. Any financial transaction exceeding 50 dinars must be carried out with a bank card.

6. The currency brought from outside the country must necessarily be declared at customs and converted in Tunisian banks. Anyone who intentionally imports money without declaring it will be brought to justice.

7. The State sets a specific deadline, at the latest, of 3 months, for exchanging any sum of money through the bank. Any citizen who has not returned old currency, risk of prosecution. Anyone exchanging foreign currencies outside official channels (money laundering and transfer

---

[43] Speech by Habib Bourguiba, Ariha (Palestine), 1965.

of funds obtained through illegal means) will be brought to justice.

8. All organizations placed under the control of the State, such as independent constitutional bodies (independent higher body for elections, national body for the fight against corruption, national body for the protection of personal data, national body Prevention of Torture, Human Rights Body and Access to Information Body) must be subject to an annual audit. They are required to submit a detailed report of their activities as well as cases handled, including those related to sums looted by former politicians, businessmen and members of the Ennahdha party who have obtained billions of dinars compensations. As such, any person responsible for the stripping of public funds from the start of the revolution will be brought to justice.

9. The President of the Republic must issue a presidential decree to the Assembly of People's Representatives to reduce the salaries of deputies for a period of 3 years, as well as for his own salary as well as that of the ministers.

10. The Tunisian state must return the administrative cars that require expensive maintenance (in addition to fuel costs), which will save 200 billion to 320 billion Tunisian dinars.

11. The governor should be appointed according to the region to which he belongs. The governor in office is required to inspect all disadvantaged areas at all times (supply water and electricity, check the condition of roads and rural schools, an inventory of poor families to provide them with food, clothing and blankets). He will have to submit a monthly report to the Prime Minister and then to the President of the Republic on the state of affairs of all the regions.

12. Charitable organizations and civil society are required to submit a monthly report to the governor, who in turn must be required to report it to the relevant public authorities.

13. Auditing of the accounts of all private sector companies should be scheduled. All businesses, Tunisian and foreign factories operating in Tunisia, must pay taxes within 6 months, including businesses and restaurants. Beyond this date, risk of legal action.

14. Provide in any business or administration training on the impact of corporate culture and social ties on economic productivity. All employees must be made aware of the collective benefits and the added values of motivation, quality and attendance at work.

15. Identify all officials who are responsible for funds in banks, movable and immovable property. In the same way, in the form of external audits, supervise all civil servants who occupy positions of responsibility in the public service, in order to prevent possible implications in corruption cases.

16. Organize subcontracting collaborations between public companies (Tunisian electricity and gas company -STEG- and national water exploitation and distribution company -SONEDE), and small companies in the 3rd sector of the ESS.

17. The revenues of the Phosphate company Gafsa, must be distributed in an equitable way between the regions, under the aegis of the referent ministry of the ESS.

18. Anyone who is unemployed will receive 250 dinars per month, until a job is obtained through the public or private sector. Young people (20 to 30 years old, girls and boys) who are unemployed, may be assigned to the Ministry of Defense or the Ministry of the Interior.

19. Small enterprises play a strong role in the development strategy of many countries, and their importance is undeniable in Tunisia. However, access to financing is a major obstacle for them, which CUR'ESS could remedy by presenting financial alternatives that are parallel to banking circuits and more flexible.

20. The Central Bank of Tunisia, the keystone of its economic system, must become a more transparent institution, through its functions and methods to control the banks as well as to finance the economic and social sectors. Civil society and SSE institutions could, in a participatory manner, become a force for advice or proposals in order to stabilize the 3rd sector.

CONCLUSION

Since February 2020, we have only been talking about the « Corona » virus and medical isolation, which is sweeping the world at very high speed. Before the rest of the world, the countries most affected were China, Italy, Spain and France.

The number of infections and death rates are on the rise, waves of lockdowns follow one another, and countries do not always reveal the right numbers. Vaccines are developing at different rates depending on the country, advocated as the miracle solution but without any temporal hindsight on their side effects.

The virus has weakened individuals and groups, it has developed and almost institutionalized social distancing, it has succeeded in transmitting fear and anguish through the media and governments around the world. Without distinguishing between North and South, however, it makes the poor and the destitute more vulnerable.

This epidemic is to date without real origin. Those who are worried point to the mutation of a virus during handling in Chinese laboratories that have reportedly managed to hide the case. Those who doubt accuse, just like China, the United States of having spread this virus through a group of soldiers who underwent military training in Wuhan in October 2019. Those who believe in it defend the thesis origin of the fish market in the Chinese city of Wuhan, the consumption of pangolins and their crossing with bats.

At the center of the debate over the origins could be found in the trade war now waged between the two countries vying for world leadership. The United States, whose president has confined himself to selfish and protectionist denial of the seriousness of the epidemic, could be the big losers. As for China, its aid to the countries most affected during the first wave, and its apparent effectiveness in resolving the crisis on its national territory, were able to distinguish it in the eyes of the world.

This crisis is presented as an indicator of the geopolitics of the world and the establishment of a new international order. The virus has hit global commerce and its focus on China's digital and pharmaceutical industries. China is the factory of the world. She stopped for a few months but has so far made a good start. It will not reduce its exports, but will Europe and the United States choose protectionism, suspend their imports, reorganize and relocate their productions, and rearrange their markets ? The difficulty of moving, importing and exporting could lead many countries to bet on reviving their own resources in order to guarantee the needs of their populations, and therefore to ensure their national security. Will consumption drop, and how will international trade be affected ?

Such a pause on the part of its partners would strike the Chinese economy deeply in its ambition to become the world's greatest economic power. However, it is possible that nothing will change and that China, having regulated the pandemic, is in a position to retake all the markets and gain new ones, particularly in southern and developing countries. While the United States, entangled in a deplorable management centered on the sole personality of its president and mobilized by a social and cultural crisis (treatment police officer of black minorities), will have to build a slow resilience.

The epidemic can be seen as a great paradox signaling the end of globalization: a virus that circulates across borders, and unlike countries that close their doors and turn in on themselves. Globalization to date has relied mainly on free trade, free movement of capital and investment, and ease of communication between countries. Logically, will each company pay for the revival of its skills and its regional and local industries ? Will Tunisia then have to refocus on its heritage and on its cultural tourism ?

For this, we are proposing a reorientation of its development towards a third sector energized by our « Curriculum of the social and solidarity economy » (CUR'ESS). This is a first solution to significantly reduce the spread of poverty, hunger, monopoly and money laundering by transforming the informal sector and parallel commerce into an organized sector based on partnership, promotion of entrepreneurship, reduction of unemployment. This sector would be fueled by the production of income-generating activities that would make it possible to exit an informal economy, then would help to encourage the production of local products (agricultural products, etc.) to achieve self-sufficiency, and reduce dependence in relation to the State.

To do this, Tunisia will certainly have to situate itself by reference to the new international order described in this essay: the history of its alliances with the United States and its allies in the Middle East, its political and financial corruption at the top of the world. 'State, the fight against petty corruption and informal practices, the restructuring of its social and solidarity economy within a third sector in dialogue with the public and private sectors. In the light of the pandemic that is setting in, she will then have to also initiate its coronavirage between the social, the economic and the political. This announced turning point for Tunisian society, in the coming months and in connection with the monitoring of the pandemic, will be the subject of a forthcoming work.

BIBLIOGRAPHY

Raymond Barre, « L'économie de la Tunisie : problèmes et perspectives », *IBLA*, vol. 17, n°67, 1954.

B.M. Bhatia, *Famines in India: a study in some aspects of the economic history of India, 1860-1945*, Asia Publishing House, 1963.

Giorgio Blundo, Jean-Pierre Olivier de Sardan, « Introduction. Étudier la corruption quotidienne : pourquoi et comment ? », Dans *État et corruption en Afrique*, 2007, pp 5-28.

Andreas Von Bülow, *Die CIA und der 11 septembre. Internationaler Terror und die Rolle der Geheimdienste*, Piper Verlag GmbH, Munich, 2003

Khalifa Chater, « La Franc-maçonnerie en Tunisie à l'épreuve de la colonisation (1930-1956) », *Cahiers de la Méditerranée*, 72 | 2006, pp 367-375.

Pierre-Noel Denieuil, Houda Laroussi, *Tunisie 2011-2014. Radioscopie d'une entrée en révolution*, L'Harmattan, Paris, 2017

Pierre-Noel Denieuil, *Le chercheur, le diplomate et la révolution tunisienne - Mémoires d'un directeur d'Institut français en Tunisie (2008-2013)*, Paris, L'Harmattan, 2016.

Cyrille Devendeville, « Les aspects généraux de la mutualisation », *Gazette des archives*, pp. 33-40, 2013.

Bernard Eme & Jean-Louis Laville, *Cohésion sociale et emploi,* Paris, Desclée de Brouwer, 1994.

Song Hongjing, *La Guerre des monnaies. La Chine et le Nouvel Ordre mondial*, Editions Le Retour aux Sources, Paris, 2013.

David Jarry, « Le Dr. Eric Pianka déclarait en 2006 à l'Université du Texas : l'utilisation de Ebola permettrait d'exterminer 90% de la population mondiale », publié le 1octobre 2014, Webmaster. URL : http://conscience-du-peuple.blogspot.com/2012/01/le-scientifique-dr-eric-r-pianka-defend.html

Henry Kissinger, *L'ordre du monde*, Fayard, Paris, 2016

Houda Laroussi, *Micro-crédit et lien social. La solidarité instituée*, Editions Karthala, Paris, 2009

Houda Laroussi, « L'économie sociale et solidaire. Une approche tunisienne », plateforme

Chabaka.tn : https://urlz.fr/bMNM, 7 février, 2020

Imed Melliti et Hayet Moussa (dir.), *Quand les jeunes parlent d'injustice. Expériences, registres et mots en Tunisie* ; préface de Sihem Najar, L'Harmattan, Paris, 2018

Sihem Najar, *Les réseaux sociaux sur Internet à l'heure des transitions démocratiques*, Paris, Karthala, 2013

Lisa Roméo, « Déclaration Balfour », publié le 11 septembre 2010, URL : https://www.lesclesdumoyenorient.com/Declaration-Balfour.html

Syed Ali Salman, « Banque islamique dans la région du Moyen-Orient et de l'Afrique du Nord (MENA) », Islamic Economic Studies, The Islamic Research and Training Institute (IRTI), vol. 20, pages 1-44, 2012.

Jean-Michel Servet, interview par Philippe Le Bé, « Coronavirus ? C'est une fois de plus sauve qui peut les banques », Bilan, 6 avril 2020. https://www.bilan.ch/finance/coronavirus-cest-une-fois-de-plus-sauve-qui-peut-la-finance

Jean-Michel Servet, « Coronavirus : une opportunité pour une politique monétaire au bénéfice de tous », Le Temps, 24 mars 2020 avec Solène Morvant-Roux.

https://www.letemps.ch/economie/coronavirus-une-opportunite-une-politique-monetaire-benefice

Frank Snowden, *Epidemics and Society: From the Black Death to the Present*, Yale University Press, 2019. URL : https://yalebooks.yale.edu/book/9780300192216/epidemics-and-society

Stephen Taylor, *The Psychology of Pandemics: Preparing for the Next Global Outbreak of Infectious Disease*, Cambridge Scholars Publishing, 2019.

Roger Le Tourneau, « Le Maghreb d'antan a-t-il connu des révolutions ?», *Revue des mondes musulmans et de la Méditerranée*, 1968, pp. 153-160

REPORTS

La petite corruption : le danger banalisé. Étude exploratoire sur la petite corruption en Tunisie. Publication du rapport de l'ATCP, Association tunisienne des contrôleurs publics, 2015

CONSULTING SITE

« Coronavirus: cinq épidémies qui ont contribué à changer le cours de l'histoire ». https://www.bbc.com/afrique/monde-52076467

Tribune, « Coronavirus : la crise pourrait mettre au chômage 25 millions de personnes dans le monde », 18 mars 2020. https://www.latribune.fr/economie/international/coronavirus-la-crise-pourrait-mettre-au-chomage-25-millions-de-personnes-dans-le-monde-842616.html

http://www.espaces-latinos.org/archives/90174

https://fr.wikipedia.org/wiki/Fajr_Libya

https://en.wikipedia.org/wiki/Qatar_Fund_for_Development

https://en.wikipedia.org/wiki/Death_by_China

https://www.lemonde.fr/economie/article/2020/05/08/aux-etats-unis-le-taux-de-chomage-au-plus-haut-depuis-50-ans_6039101_3234.html.

https://www.franceinter.fr/vie-quotidienne/boris-cyrulnik-apres-le-coronavirus-il-y-aura-des-changements-profonds-c-est-la-regle

https://fr.wikipedia.org/wiki/La_Guerre_des_monnaies._La_Chine_et_le_Nouvel_Ordre_mondial

TABLE OF CONTENTS

Dans la collection
Socio-anthropologie des mondes méditerranéens et africains

Houda Laroussi, *La Tunisie en pandémie. De la corruption à la solidarité*, L'Harmattan, Paris, 2021.

Halima Ouanada (dir.), *(Re)penser le féminin*, L'Harmattan, Paris, 2020.

Mohamed Jouili, Maryam Ben Salem (dir.), *Engagement citoyen et jeunesse plurielle en Tunisie*, L'Harmattan, Paris, 2020.

Soumaya Abdellatif, *De l'adoption en Tunisie. Controverses filiales*, L'Harmattan, Paris, 2020.

Sihem Najar, Lilia Othman Challougui (dir.), *Écrire sur les jeunes. Des réalités juvéniles questionnées par la jeune recherche en Tunisie*, L'Harmattan, Paris, 2019.

Abdelfettah Benchenna, Hélène Bourdeloie et Zineb Majdouli (dir.), *Cultures et jeunes adultes en région Méditerranée. Circulations, pratiques et soft power*, L'Harmattan, Paris, 2019.

Salma Derouiche-El Kamel, *Narcissisme, corps et création. L'artiste à l'épreuve de la projection*, L'Harmattan, Paris, 2019.

Régine Tchicaya-Oboa, *Femmes créatrices d'entreprises au Congo-Brazzaville. 10 portraits*, L'Harmattan, Paris, 2018.

Imed Melliti, Hayet Moussa (dir.), *Quand les jeunes parlent d'injustice. Expériences, registres et mots en Tunisie*, L'Harmattan, Paris, 2018.

Yassine Akhiate, *L'audiovisuel au Maroc en 10 questions*, L'Harmattan, Paris, 2018.

Youssef Sadik, *Les paradoxes de l'employabilité dans les pays du Sud. Le travail et l'entreprise à l'épreuve de la mondialisation*, L'Harmattan, Paris, 2018.

Houda Laroussi, *Femmes et développement local en Tunisie. Acteurs et enjeux*. L'Harmattan, Paris, 2018.

Houda Laroussi (dir.), *Pratiques du travail social en France et au Maghreb. Compétences, formation et professionnalisation.* L'Harmattan, Paris, 2017.

Aïssa Merah, Michèle Gellereau et Nabila Aldjia Bouchaala (dir.), *Reconfiguration des expressions et des pratiques culturelles à l'ère du numérique en Méditerranée*. L'Harmattan, Paris, 2017.

Pierre-Noël Denieuil et Houda Laroussi, *Tunisie 2011-2014. Radioscopie d'une entrée en révolution*. L'Harmattan, Paris, 2017.

Nadia Kerdoud, *Recompositions urbaines et nouveaux espaces de consommation en Algérie. Les dynamiques commerciales aux périphéries des villes de l'Est algérien*. L'Harmattan, Paris, 2017.

Pierre-Noël Denieuil, *Le chercheur, le diplomate et la révolution tunisienne. Mémoires d'un directeur d'Institut français en Tunisie (2008-2013)*. L'Harmattan, Paris, 2016.

Abdelfettah Benchenna et Luc Pinhas (dir.), *Industries culturelles et entrepreneuriat au Maghreb*. L'Harmattan, Paris, 2016.

Racha Meziou et Zeineb Cherni (dir.), *Usages des technologies numériques de l'information et de la communication : constructions identitaires et interculturalités*. GDRI CNRS et L'Harmattan, Paris, 2015.

Sihem Najar et Lilia Othman Challougui (dir.), *Ecrire sur les femmes. Retour réflexif sur une expérience de recherche*. CAWTAR et L'Harmattan, Tunis/Paris, 2014.

Sihem Najar (dir.), *Nouvelles technologies et lien social en Méditerranée*. GDRI CNRS et L'Harmattan, Tunis, Paris, 2014.

Nadhem YOUSFI, *Des Tunisiens dans les Alpes-Maritimes : une histoire locale et nationale de la migration transméditerranéenne*. IRMC-L'Harmattan, Paris, 2013.

Ridha BEN AMOR, *Les formes élémentaires du lien social en Tunisie. De l'entraide à la reconnaissance*. IRMC-L'Harmattan, Paris, 2011.

Odile MOREAU (dir.), *Réforme de l'Etat et réformismes au Maghreb (XIXe-XXe siècles)*. IRMC-L'Harmattan, Paris, 2009.

Structures éditoriales du groupe L'Harmattan

L'Harmattan Italie
Via degli Artisti, 15
10124 Torino
harmattan.italia@gmail.com

L'Harmattan Hongrie
Kossuth l. u. 14-16.
1053 Budapest
harmattan@harmattan.hu

L'Harmattan Sénégal
10 VDN en face Mermoz
BP 45034 Dakar-Fann
senharmattan@gmail.com

L'Harmattan Cameroun
TSINGA/FECAFOOT
BP 11486 Yaoundé
inkoukam@gmail.com

L'Harmattan Burkina Faso
Achille Somé – tengnule@hotmail.fr

L'Harmattan Guinée
Almamya, rue KA 028 OKB Agency
BP 3470 Conakry
harmattanguinee@yahoo.fr

L'Harmattan RDC
185, avenue Nyangwe
Commune de Lingwala – Kinshasa
matangilamusadila@yahoo.fr

L'Harmattan Congo
67, boulevard Denis-Sassou-N'Guesso
BP 2874 Brazzaville
harmattan.congo@yahoo.fr

L'Harmattan Mali
ACI 2000 - Immeuble Mgr Jean Marie Cisse
Bureau 10
BP 145 Bamako-Mali
mali@harmattan.fr

L'Harmattan Togo
Djidjole – Lomé
Maison Amela
face EPP BATOME
ddamela@aol.com

L'Harmattan Côte d'Ivoire
Résidence Karl – Cité des Arts
Abidjan-Cocody
03 BP 1588 Abidjan
espace_harmattan.ci@hotmail.fr

Nos librairies en France

Librairie internationale
16, rue des Écoles
75005 Paris
librairie.internationale@harmattan.fr
01 40 46 79 11
www.librairieharmattan.com

Librairie des savoirs
21, rue des Écoles
75005 Paris
librairie.sh@harmattan.fr
01 46 34 13 71
www.librairieharmattansh.com

Librairie Le Lucernaire
53, rue Notre-Dame-des-Champs
75006 Paris
librairie@lucernaire.fr
01 42 22 67 13

www.ingramcontent.com/pod-product-compliance
Lightning Source LLC
LaVergne TN
LVHW010054061026
849532LV00004BC/1516